She Would Not Be Moved

Also by Herbert Kohl

The Age of Complexity
36 Children
The Open Classroom
View from the Oak (with Judith Kohl)
Growing with Your Children
Growing Minds: On Becoming a Teacher
From Archetype to Zeitgeist: An Essential Guide to Powerful Ideas
"I Won't Learn from You"
Should We Burn Babar?
The Discipline of Hope
Stupidity and Tears

She Would Not Be Moved

How We Tell the Story of Rosa Parks and the Montgomery Bus Boycott

HERBERT KOHL

INTRODUCTION BY MARIAN WRIGHT EDELMAN

THE NEW PRESS

NEW YORK
LONDON

Requests for permission to reproduce selections from this book should be mailed to:
Permissions Department, The New Press, 120 Wall Street, 31st floor, New York, NY 10005

First published in the United States by The New Press, New York, 2005
This paperback edition published by The New Press, 2007
Distributed by Perseus Distribution

ISBN 978-1-59558-127-3 (pbk.)

LIBRARY OF CONGRESS CATALOGING-IN-PUBLICATION DATA

Kohl, Herbert R.
   She would not be moved : how we tell the story of Rosa Parks and the
Montgomery bus boycott / Herbert Kohl ; introduction by Marian Wright
Edelman.
      p. cm.
   Includes the following essay: Close bonds / by Cynthia Brown.
   Includes bibliographical references and index.
   ISBN 978-1-59558-020-7
   1. Parks, Rosa, 1913– 2. African American women civil rights workers—
Alabama—Montgomery—Biography—History and criticism. 3. Civil rights
workers—Alabama—Montgomery—Biography—History and criticism. 4.
African Americans—Civil rights—Alabama—Montgomery—History—20th
century—Study and teaching (Elementary) 5. Civil rights movements—
Alabama—Montgomery—History—20th century—Study and teaching
(Elementary) 6. Segregation in transportation—Alabama—Montgomery—
History—20th century—Study and teaching (Elementary) 7. Montgomery
(Ala.)—Race relations—Study and teaching (Elementary)   I. Brown, Cynthia
Stokes.   II. Huggins, Nathan Irvin, 1927–   III. Title.

F334.M753P375   2005
323'.092—dc22
[B]   2005043882

The New Press publishes books that promote and enrich public discussion and understanding of
the issues vital to our democracy and to a more equitable world. These books are made possible
by the enthusiasm of our readers; the support of a committed group of donors, large and small;
the collaboration of our many partners in the independent media and the not-for-profit sector;
booksellers, who often hand-sell New Press books; librarians; and above all by our authors.

www.thenewpress.com

Composition by Westchester Book Composition

Printed in the United States of America

2 4 6 8 10 9 7 5 3

To the African American Community in Montgomery, Alabama

Our times seem to call for new myths and a revised master narrative that better inspire and reflect our true condition. . . . Such a new narrative would bring slavery and the persistent oppression of race from the margins to the center, to define the limits and the boundaries of the American Dream. Such a new narrative would oblige us to face the deforming mirror of truth.

—Nathan Irvin Huggins,
Revelations: American History, American Myths

Contents

Acknowledgments

There are many people who contributed to the making of this book, but one person, Myles Horton, founder of the Highlander Center, got me thinking about retelling stories in ways that reflect what he would have called reality on the ground. Through Highlander I had the opportunity to meet Rosa Parks several times and learn of her extraordinary strength, intelligence, and determination. Before learning about her through Highlander, I too had been a victim of the "Rosa Was Tired" myth. As an educator, I knew how deeply this myth, which portrays the Montgomery bus boycott as a spontaneous action based simply on anger and frustration, is embedded in what we teach children about the struggle for civil rights. The story of the power of the community and the sophisticated planning that went into making a successful boycott was neglected or invisible. So I decided to begin with the myth and reconstruct it to get closer to the truth about the bold, thoughtful, and collective actions that enabled the Montgomery, Alabama, African American community to confront a dangerous, segregationist white community and win.

In developing this reconstruction many other people have provided resources and insights. First, of course, is my wife,

Judy, and then there are many of my students from Hamline University in St. Paul who helped by reading school texts and young people's books to uncover the extent of the myth. I also want to thank my colleague, Ilkwon Shingo Hwang, who helped update the references to texts and children's books. Finally, there is Robert Silvers, editor of the *New York Review of Books,* whose letter critiquing an early draft of this book contributed to what I hope is an improvement of my arguments and documentation.

I owe a special thanks to my friend and longtime colleague Cynthia Brown for her insights, conversation, and support. In addition, I am more than grateful for the wonderful essay she wrote specifically for this book that provides insights into the development of Rosa Parks as an activist.

Special thanks are due to my editor, Diane Wachtell, who convinced me to turn an earlier essay on Rosa Parks and the bus boycott into this work. She guided me through the process and is, as always, a pleasure to work with, as is her assistant, Joel Ariaratnam. My agent, Wendy Weil, also provided insights into the text and supported and consoled me when deadlines and other details seemed overwhelming. Wendy's support always keeps me going.

Finally, I must acknowledge the work and lives of the people who planned and made effective the Montgomery bus boycott. They are the ones who took all the risks: Rosa Parks, E.D. Nixon, Jo Anne Robinson, Martin Luther King Jr., and the thousands of African American citizens who boycotted the buses and who, through their actions, made the United States a more democratic nation.

Introduction

Marian Wright Edelman

I am so grateful for this book. Rosa Parks's story is one all children need to know, and Herbert Kohl is so right to insist we learn how to teach our children the *correct* history of what led up to that December day on the Montgomery bus. They need to know, as the saying goes, "the rest of the story." Putting Mrs. Parks's story in its full context allows children to get a much fuller sense of the kinds of planned activism and community action that happened in small towns and larger cities across the South during the Civil Rights Movement. It's important for them to know that courageous leaders like Rosa Parks and Martin Luther King Jr. didn't suddenly appear out of nowhere, and that they weren't superhumans with magical powers. They were ordinary people, just like all of the other parents, neighbors, and ministers in the community, and like all of the familiar adults in our children's lives today. But they became heroes and made history because they were willing to stand up and make a difference. Teaching children this lesson reinforces the idea that *they* can make a difference too.

Even better, when we are committed to teaching children the full story of the Civil Rights Movement, we can also tell them about Ruby Bridges and the Little Rock Nine, and boys and girls like the children in the Carter family who integrated their Mississippi schools, or the children who stood up to police with fire hoses in Birmingham and brought down the walls of racial oppression—and show them the key role children just like themselves played. These children were moral witnesses for America, and the world, and helped push our nation to do the right things. They are one of the most important testaments in American history to the fact that *you are never too young to make a difference.*

It's also crucial for our children to learn that Rosa Parks was a strong woman with a plan to fight for what she believed in so that both boys and girls will understand she is part of a rich history of women's activism. Even today, sometimes we still need to remind our children that not all of the heroes of American history are white or male. And in every major American and progressive political social reform movement, women have always played a critical role. Many times they are in the background, employing quiet leadership and organizational, communication, and fundraising skills—but often they are at the forefront, acting as the catalyst for progress when it needs to happen. The quest for a better world has been, and is, the daily work of thousands upon thousands of women everywhere. We are not afraid to change things.

I have a special respect for Rosa Parks because I grew up surrounded by women like her in my own hometown of Bennettsville, South Carolina. I was so blessed to grow up in a household with a true partnership between a mother and father, who taught me how to organize and mobilize communities and help keep institutions running. They both made it clear that my sister and I were expected to achieve as much as or more than my three older brothers. My father was the pastor of our Baptist church, and my mother was a true leader and entrepreneur—the choir director, church organist, founder and head of the Mothers' Club, a pillar of the missionary society. The church could not have run without her and the circle of formidable women she organized, just as most churches and religious institutions would collapse today without women who provide the quiet human infrastructure to keep them going. Few of our other community organizations could have run without these women either. Women are quite often the glue that holds together not only our homes, but our congregations, institutions, and communities.

The black women who ran my church and community had much in common with Rosa Parks and the other women who were such an integral part of the Civil Rights Movement, many of whom are still unsung heroines in our children's textbooks. I'm so glad this book will remind children of the role Jo Ann Robinson played in leading the planning for the Montgomery bus boycott. At many points during the Civil Rights Movement, Martin Luther King Jr. would have been a reactor responding to events had Ella Baker not set up an infrastructure to anticipate, catalyze, and help shape them. If Septima Clark had not set up citizenship schools there would not have been a vehicle for doing voter registration. Women such as Dr. Dorothy Height, Fannie Lou Hamer, Mae Bertha Carter, and Diane Nash were the backbone of the Civil Rights Movement; the list goes on and on.

There are so many stories to tell. In getting *this* story right,

Herb Kohl sets an example for how much is to be gained by paying attention to all of the details every time we teach history, and her story. He also elevates Rosa Parks's true activism to its correct stature, which it so richly deserves. He lays out a clear, engaging, and accurate method for introducing children to one of our national role models and treasures. I hope many parents and teachers will learn something new about the Rosa Parks story from this book, and that they, like the children who will be hearing it, will be deeply inspired.

She Would Not Be Moved

1

She Would Not Be Moved

Racism, and the direct confrontation between African American and European American people in the United States, is an issue that is usually considered too sensitive to be dealt with directly in the elementary school classroom. When African Americans and European Americans are involved in confrontation in children's literature, the situation is routinely described as a problem between individuals that can be worked out on a personal basis. In the few cases where racism is addressed as a social problem, there has to be a happy ending with a hero or heroine but without any adversaries. The civil rights literature for children is devoid of specific white individuals who are racist and do horrible things to black people. It is, one might say, "whitewashed." In addition, the traditions of community solidarity, risk taking, and organizing in black communities are passed over in silence. These circumstances are most readily apparent in the usual biographical treatments of Rosa Parks, one of the two individuals whom most children in the United States associate with the Civil Rights Movement in the South during the 1960s, the other being Martin Luther King Jr.

Over the past few years, when I've made school visits, I've talked with children about the Civil Rights Movement. One of the things I ask them is what they know about Rosa Parks and her involvement in the Montgomery bus boycott. This focus developed after I observed a play about civil rights in a fourth-grade classroom in Southern California several years ago. One scene in the play took place on a bus in Montgomery, Alabama. A tired Rosa Parks got on the bus and sat down. The child portraying Mrs. Parks was dressed in shabby clothes and carried two worn shopping bags. She sat down next to the driver and then other children got on the bus until all the seats in the front were filled. Then a boy got on and asked her to move. She refused, and so the bus driver told her he didn't want any trouble and politely asked her to move to the back of the bus. She refused again and the scene ended. In the next scene we see a crowd of students, African American and European American, carrying signs saying, "Don't Ride the Buses," "We Shall Overcome," and "Blacks and Whites Together." One of the students, playing Martin Luther King Jr., addressed the rest of the class, saying something to the effect that African American and European American people in Montgomery got angry because Rosa Parks was arrested for not moving to the back of the bus, and that they were boycotting the buses until all people could sit wherever they wanted. The play ended with a narrator pointing out that the bus problem in Montgomery was solved by people coming together to protest peacefully for justice.

Before talking to the children about their perceptions of Rosa Parks and her motivations, I had a moment to talk with the teacher about a major misrepresentation of the facts in the play: there were no European Americans involved in boy-cotting the buses in Montgomery. The struggle was organized and maintained by the African American community and to represent it as an interracial struggle was to take the power and credit away from that community. The teacher agreed that the play took some liberties with history but said that since his class was interracial it was better for all of the children to do the play as an integrated struggle. Otherwise, he said, the play might lead to racial strife in the classroom. I disagreed and pointed out that by showing the power of organized African Americans, it might lead all of the children to recognize and appreciate the strength that oppressed people can demonstrate when confronting their oppressors. In addition, the fact that European Americans joined the struggle later on could lead to very interesting discussions about social change and the strug-gle for justice, and could be related to the struggles in South Africa; the release of Nelson Mandela; and to his election as president of the new nation, the Republic of South Africa. It also could be related to the resurgence of overt racism in the United States and to other forms of intolerance and group ha-tred. He disagreed and ended our chat by telling me how hard it was to manage an integrated classroom.

I contented myself with asking the children about Rosa Parks. Anna, the girl who played Mrs. Parks, told me that she imagined "Rosa," as she called Mrs. Parks, to be a poor woman who did tiring and unpleasant work. She added that she imag-ined Rosa was on her way home to a large family that she had to take care of all by herself when she refused to move to the back of the bus. In other words, Rosa Parks was, in her mind, a poor, single parent with lots of children, and an unskilled worker. I asked her how she got that idea, and she replied that it is just the kind of person she felt Rosa Parks must be. She added that nobody had ever told her that her view was wrong, so she never bothered to question it. Her teacher backed her up and claimed that she had made reasonable assumptions about Rosa Parks, ones that he felt were true to the way Rosa Parks was portrayed in the books they had in the classroom. I couldn't argue with that last comment. Nor at the moment could I argue that stereotypes and prejudices were insinuated into his curriculum under the guise of tolerance and "brotherhood."

Recently, I've talked to a number of young people about Rosa Parks and the Civil Rights Movement. Many of the students, especially the ones who were not African American, expressed puzzlement about the whole question of needing a Civil Rights Movement. They had no concept of the legalized, institutionalized racism, organized racist groups, and personal hatreds faced by African American people that created the need for a liberation movement. Their teachers told me they didn't want to stir up the problems that they anticipated would arise if they spoke too directly about white racism. Yet, there is no way to understand racism if there are no racists and no people who create and support institutionalized racism in the mix. As I recently heard Manning Marable (a leading public intellectual and professor at Columbia University) say during an interview, the story of oppression has to be shown as part of the story of freedom.

I didn't bring up the issue with Anna, but instead asked her how Rosa Parks's arrest led to a bus boycott. She said she didn't know. Maybe Rosa had a friend who told everybody, or maybe it was in the newspaper. One of the other students suggested that her arrest was on TV and everybody came out to protest because they didn't think it was right to arrest someone just for not moving to the back of the bus. The boycott was, to them, some form of spontaneous action that did not involve planning or strategy.

All of the children admired Rosa Parks for not moving to the back of the bus. Some said she must be a very stubborn person, others felt that she had to be so angry that she didn't care what happened to her. They agreed that it took a special person to be so courageous and wondered if they would be able to muster such courage. I got the impression that Mrs. Parks's exceptional courage might be an excuse for them not to act.

I decided to push the issue a bit and asked the class why Rosa Parks had to move to the back of the bus anyway. One of the African American children said it was segregated in the South back then, and African Americans and European Americans couldn't do things together. When I asked why there was segregation there was absolute silence. I shifted a bit and asked if the African Americans and European Americans in their classroom could do things together. One of the boys answered, "In school they do, mostly," and since I was just a guest I left it at that. It was clear to me, however, that issues of racial conflict were not explicitly discussed in this classroom, and that the play about the Montgomery bus boycott left the children with some vague sense of unity and victory, but with no sense of the risk and courage of the African American people who originated the struggle for civil rights in the United States or of the history and nature of segregation. I have no idea whether there was any racism manifest in the everyday lives of the children in that classroom, but wondered whether they or the teacher were at all prepared to deal with it if it erupted.

The children's visualization of Rosa Parks, whom they felt free to call by her first name, was particularly distressing. They imagined her as poor, without education or sophistication, a person who acted on impulse and emotion rather than with intelligence and moral conviction. There was no sense of her as a community leader or as part of an organized struggle against oppression. I decided to find out how common this view is and have been astonished to find that those children's view of Rosa Parks is not at all different from that of most European American adults and almost all of the school children I have questioned, first in 1994, and again in 2004, when I asked the same questions of a number of students in high school classes and received the same responses.

It might even be that some of the descriptions of Rosa Parks by civil rights leaders inadvertently contributed to these misconceptions. For example, in 1966, Martin Luther King Jr. said, "After finishing my schooling, I was called to a little church down in Montgomery, Alabama. I started preaching there, things were going well in that church, it was a marvelous experience. But one day a year later a lady by the name of Rosa Parks decided she wasn't going to take it any longer. She stayed on a bus seat. It was the beginning of a movement where fifty thousand black men and women refused to ride the city buses, and we walked together 381 days."

The image of "Rosa Was Tired," and the story that goes with it, exist as a national cultural icon in the United States. Even though there are a number of recent books that represent the genesis of the Montgomery bus boycott in historically accurate ways, school textbooks have not caught up with the facts. They change much more slowly than children's books and adult literature and are often not replaced for years. In addition, many children's books still in print are major perpetuators of this myth. None of these books quote sources for their distorted personal information about Mrs. Parks, and yet, most American children's first encounter with the Civil Rights Movement comes through these writings. Dozens of children's books and textbooks I've looked at present the same version of Rosa Parks and the Montgomery bus boycott. This version can be reduced to the following generic story, which I put together[1] and could be titled:

Rosa Was Tired: The Story of the Montgomery Bus Boycott

Rosa Parks was a poor seamstress. She lived in Montgomery, Alabama, during the 1950s. Those days there was still segregation in parts of the United States. That meant that African Americans and European Americans were not allowed to use the same public facilities such as

---

[1] See the note on references at the end of this chapter for the specific sources I drew on to create this generic version of Rosa Parks's story.

restaurants or swimming pools. It also meant that when-ever it was crowded on the city buses, African Ameri-cans had to give up their seats in the front of the bus to European Americans and move to the back of the bus.

One day on her way home from work, Rosa was tired and sat down in the front of the bus. As the bus got crowded, she was asked to give up her seat to a European American man and she refused. The bus driver told her she had to go to the back of the bus, and she still refused to move. It was a hot day, and she was tired and angry and became very stubborn.

The driver called a policeman, who arrested Rosa.

When other African Americans in Montgomery heard this, they became angry too. So they decided to refuse to ride the buses until everyone was allowed to ride together. They boycotted the buses.

The boycott, which was led by Martin Luther King Jr., succeeded. Now African Americans and European Ameri-cans can ride the buses together in Montgomery.

Rosa Parks was a very brave person.

This story seems innocent enough. Rosa Parks is treated with respect and dignity and the African American community is given credit for running the boycott and winning the struggle. It reflects the view of Mrs. Parks often found in adult literature as well as in writings for children. For example, in the eminent psychiatrist Robert Coles's book *The Moral Life of Children* (Boston: Houghton Mifflin, 1986), we find the following quote:

A community meeting at the time of the boycott, illustrating the depth of community support for the struggle. (Time and Life Pictures/Getty Images)

We had come to know . . . a group of poor and poorly ed-
ucated people, who, nevertheless, acquitted themselves
impressively in pursuit of significant ethical objectives. I
think of Rosa Parks, a seamstress, whose decision to sit
where she pleased on a Montgomery, Alabama, bus in the
middle 1950s preceded the emergence of the so-called
Civil Rights Movement and of Dr. King and Ralph Abernathy as leaders of it. (p. 25)

A more recent example of this can be found in Robert Fulghum's best-selling book *It Was on Fire When I Lay Down on It*:

I write this on the first day of December in 1988, the anniversary of a moment when someone sat still and lit the
fuse to social dynamite. On this day in 1955, a forty-two-
year-old woman was on her way home from work. Getting
on a public bus, she paid her fare and sat down on the first
vacant seat. It was good to sit down—her feet were tired.
As the bus filled with passengers, the driver turned and
told her to give up her seat and move on back in the bus.
She sat still. The driver got up and shouted, "MOVE IT!"
She sat still. Passengers grumbled, cursed her, pushed at
her. Still she sat. So the driver got off the bus, called
the police, and they came to haul her off to jail and into
history.
    Rosa Parks. Not an activist or a radical. Just a quiet,
conservative, churchgoing woman with a nice family and a
decent job as a seamstress. For all the eloquent phrases that

have been turned about her place in the flow of history, she did not get on that bus looking for trouble or trying to make a statement. Going home was all she had in mind, like everybody else. She was anchored to her seat by her own dignity. Rosa Parks simply wasn't going to be a "nigger" for anybody anymore. And all she knew to do was to sit still.

(Robert Fulghum, *It Was on Fire When I Lay Down on It* [New York: Villard Books, 1989], pp. 109–10)

And here's a textbook version of the Montgomery bus boycott story written for elementary school children. It comes from the Heath Social Studies series for elementary schools (Jeff Passe and Evangeline Nicholas, *Exploring My World* [Lexington, MA: D.C. Heath and Company, 1991], reproduced on p. 188 of the Teacher's Guide) and is similar in content to my generic tale:

When Rosa Parks rode on a bus, she had to sit all the way in the back. Her city had a law. It said black people could not sit in the front of a bus.

One day Rosa was tired. She sat in the front. The bus driver told her to move. She did not. He called the police. Rosa was put in jail.

Some citizens tried to help. One of them was Martin Luther King, Jr. The citizens decided to stop riding buses until the law was changed.

Their plan worked. The law was changed. Soon, many other unfair laws were changed. Rosa Parks led the way!

The Teacher's Guide informs teachers that "Mrs. Parks's single act brought about the desegregation of buses all over the country." In a lesson plan that refers to Rosa Parks being told to move to the back of the bus, the guide informs teachers to "Tell children they will be reading about a woman who became angry when this happened to her. She decided she was not being treated fairly, and she was not going to put up with that kind of treatment anymore. Have children read to find out how the actions of Rosa Parks helped to change the way black people were treated" (p. 188).

This textbook was published in 1991 and is likely still in use. It encourages teaching the Montgomery bus boycott as the single act of a person who was tired and angry. Intelligent and passionate opposition to racism is simply not part of the story. Racism is treated in a circumspect and indirect way. In fact, the part of the guide that deals with the Montgomery bus boycott does not mention racism at all. Instead, the problem is unfairness, a more generic and softer form of abuse that avoids dealing with the fact that the great majority of white people in Montgomery were racist and capable of being violent and cruel to maintain segregation. Thus, we have neither an adequate picture of the courage of Rosa Parks nor the intelligence and resolve of the African American community in the face of racism.

Research into the history of the Montgomery bus boycott reveals other distressing characteristics of this generic story, which misrepresents an organized and carefully planned movement for social change as a spontaneous outburst based upon frustration and anger. The following annotations on "Rosa Was

Tired" suggest that we need a new story, one more in line with the truth and directed at showing the organizational intelligence and determination of the African American community in Birmingham, as well as the role of the bus boycott in the larger struggle to desegregate Birmingham and the South.

From "Rosa Was Tired" to "Rosa Was Ready"

Given the disparity between the usual story of Rosa Parks and the Montgomery bus boycott, and the historical information that has emerged, it occurred to me that exposing the myth and retelling the story using information currently available made sense. The questions that I chose to address are: Who tells the story? and Who constructs the narrative? Here is one way to take the standard Rosa Parks story, the one I compiled from many school texts and children's books, and reconstruct it line by line in a way that pays full respect to Rosa Parks and also to the other people who made the boycott possible and most of all to the courageous African American people of Montgomery who boycotted the buses and stayed the course for more than a year.

1. *Rosa Parks was a poor seamstress. She lived in Montgomery, Alabama, during the 1950s.*

Rosa Parks was one of the first women in Montgomery to join the National Association for the Advancement of Colored

This billboard was posted throughout the South during the 1950s and 1960s. It shows Rosa Parks, Martin Luther King Jr., and Myles Horton during a meeting at the Highlander Center, the so-called "Communist Training Center." (Photograph by Dale Ernsberger, Nashville *Tennessean*)

People (NAACP) and was its secretary for years. At the NAACP she worked with E.D. Nixon, vice president of the Brotherhood of Sleeping Car Porters, who was president of the Montgomery NAACP, and learned about union struggles from him. She also worked with the youth division of the NAACP, and she took a youth NAACP group to visit the Freedom Train when it came to Montgomery in 1954. The train, which carried the original U.S. Constitution and the Declaration of Independence, was traveling around the United States promoting the virtues of democracy. Since its visit was a federal project, access to the exhibits could not be legally segregated. Mrs. Parks took advantage of that fact to visit the train. There, Rosa Parks and the members of the youth group mingled freely with European Americans from Montgomery who were also looking at the documents. This overt act of crossing the boundaries of segregation did not endear Rosa Parks to the Montgomery political and social establishment.

Her work as a seamstress in a large department store was secondary to her community work. As Rosa Parks says in an interview printed in *My Soul Is Rested* (Howell Raines [New York: Putnam, 1977], p. 35), she had "almost a life history of being rebellious against being mistreated because of my color." She was well known to all of the African American leaders in Montgomery for her opposition to segregation, her leadership abilities, and her moral strength. Since 1954 and the Supreme Court's decision in *Brown v. Board of Education of Topeka, Kansas,* she had been working on the desegregation of the Montgomery schools. In addition, she was good friends with Clifford and Virginia Durr, European Americans who

Martin Luther King Jr. and other community members at a strategy planning meeting during the Boycott. (Time and Life Pictures/Getty Images)

were well-known opponents of segregation. She also had attended an interracial meeting at the Highlander Center in Tennessee a few months before the bus boycott. Highlander was known throughout the South as a radical educational center that was overtly planning for the total desegregation of the South, and Rosa Parks was aware of that when she attended the meeting at the invitation of Virginia Durr and Septima Clark, who was the director of the Highlander Center at that time. At that meeting, which dealt with plans for school desegregation in the South, she indicated that she intended to become an active participant in other attempts to break down the barriers of segregation.

Here is Septima Clark's account of Rosa Parks's Highlander experience:

I went to Highlander twice the first summer in '54, and the following summer I used my car to transport three groups of six persons each to Highlander workshops. At the end of that summer we held a workshop to develop leadership, which I was directing. That was when I met Rosa Parks.

At that time Mrs. Parks lived in Montgomery, Alabama. Her husband was a barber, and he used to shave and cut hair for all of the high-class whites. Rosa was working with the youth group of the National Association for the Advancement of Colored People, or the N, double A, C, P, for short. . . .

We had a large group of people at the workshop. It was a two-week workshop on the United Nations. We knew that Rosa had been working with a youth group in Montgomery, so at the meeting I asked Rosa to tell how she was able to get the Freedom Train to Montgomery and get this youth group through the Freedom Train. She wouldn't talk at first.

People at the workshop knew only a little bit about the Freedom Train. It was being sent by the government around the country from Washington, D.C., as a lesson in democracy. It carried an exhibit of the original U.S. Constitution and the Declaration of Independence. Anyone could go in free but segregation was not permitted.

One night up there in the bedroom (there were about six beds in this dormitory) everyone started singing and dancing, whites kids and all, and they said, "Rosa, how in the world did you deal with that Freedom Train?"

Then she said, "It wasn't an easy task. We took our children down when the Freedom Train came, and the white and black children had to go in together. They wouldn't let them go in otherwise, and that was a real victory for us. . . ."

After the workshop, Rosa was afraid to go from Highlander to Atlanta. Myles sent me with her. She was afraid that somebody had already spoken, and she didn't know what was going to happen. I went with her to Atlanta and saw her in a bus going down to Montgomery. She felt much better then.

I guess she kept thinking about the things at the workshop. At the end of the workshops we always say, "What do you plan to do when you get back home?" Rosa answered that question by saying that Montgomery was the

From the porch of the Dexter Avenue Baptist Church you can see the
Alabama State Capitol Building, the "Capitol of the Confederacy" which
is also on Dexter Avenue. That was the building where Robert E. Lee was
inaugurated as President of the Confederacy. During Rosa Parks's time the
flag of the Confederacy was still flying over its dome. (Original illustration
from *Harper's Weekly*, March 9, 1861)

cradle of the Confederacy, that nothing would happen there because blacks wouldn't stick together. . . .

Three months after Rosa got back to Montgomery, on December 1, 1955, she refused to get up from her seat on the bus.

In addition, Rosa Parks had the active support of her mother and her husband in her civil rights activities. To call Rosa Parks a poor, tired seamstress and not talk about her role as a community leader and civil rights activist as well, is to turn an organized struggle for freedom into a personal act of frustration. It is a thorough misrepresentation of the Civil Rights Movement in Montgomery, Alabama, and an insult to Mrs. Parks as well. Here is a more appropriate way of beginning a children's version of the Montgomery bus boycott:

It was 1955. Everyone in the African American community in Montgomery, Alabama, knew Rosa Parks. She was a community leader and people admired her courage. All throughout her life she had opposed prejudice, even if it got her into trouble with European American people.

2. *Those days there was still segregation in parts of the United States. That meant that African Americans and European Americans were not allowed to use the same public facilities.*

The existence of legalized segregation in the South during the 1950s is integral to the story of the Montgomery bus boycott, yet it is an embarrassment to many school people and difficult to explain to children without accounting for the moral corruption of the majority of the European American community in the South. The sentence I composed is one way of avoiding direct confrontation with the moral issues of segregation. First, it says, "Those days there was still segregation" as if segregation were no longer an issue. However, as recently as July 1, 1990, an article by Ron Rapoport of the *Los Angeles Daily News* focused on the current segregation of private golf clubs in Birmingham and other parts of the United States. In the article he writes:

> It certainly isn't a secret that Shoal Creek Country Club has no black members because, in the words of its founder, Hall Thompson, "that's just not done in Birmingham."
>
> There are lots of places where it's just not done and not just in the South, either. Many of the golf courses that host PGA (Professional Golfers Association) events are restricted and while it may not often become a public issue, that does not mean people are not aware of it.
>
> As for shame, well, that is a commodity in short supply as well.
>
> "The country club is our home," Thompson said, "and we pick and choose who we want."
>
> (Reprinted from the Santa Rosa, CA,
Press Democrat, July 1, 1990)

To this day, the club still has only one African American member who has special status as a guest member. Ironically, in 1994,

Tiger Woods, an African American golfer, won a tournament at the club while other African Americans demonstrated outside of its gates protesting the club's segregationist policies.

That incident was more than ten years ago, but this news story was published in the *San Francisco Chronicle* on December 4, 2004 (p. A4):

Segregationist Amendment Now Leading in Alabama

(Associated Press) Montgomery, Alabama—A statewide recount showed that Alabama narrowly voted to keep language in the State Constitution supporting segregation and poll taxes, according to unofficial totals released Friday.

Even though this part of the Alabama Constitution is not enforced, the vote shows the current sentiment of a majority of white people in Alabama. The persistence of racism in Alabama is explicit, and this should provide a perspective about how courageous Rosa Parks was in the 1950s and potentially how much she had to lose by her actions.

Locating segregation in the past is a way of avoiding dealing with its current manifestations and implies that racism is no longer a major problem in the United States. This is particularly pernicious at a time when overt racism is once again becoming a common phenomenon, and children have to be helped to understand and eliminate it.

Describing integration passively ("there was still segregation"), instead of actively ("European Americans segregated facilities so that African Americans couldn't use them"), avoids the issue of active racist behavior on the part of some whites. Since there was legalized segregation in Alabama and Mrs. Parks was arrested for a violation of the Alabama state law that institutionalized segregation in public facilities, there must have been some racists who passed those laws. Yet, they are absent from the narrative, which doesn't talk overtly about racism. Avoiding direct discussion of what to do about individuals who are racist is all too characteristic of school programs and children's literature.

This avoidance is also evident in the next sentence, which says, "African Americans and European Americans were not allowed to use the same public facilities." It puts "African Americans" and "European Americans" on the same footing, as if there were some symmetry and both were punished by the segregation laws. A more appropriate way of describing the situation would be to state: "African American people were prevented by law from using the same public facilities as European Americans. In addition, the African American facilities were vastly inferior to the ones made available to European Americans."

Even this rewriting is too generous given the pervasive, brutal, and absolute nature of segregation in the pre–civil rights South. Perhaps the best analogy that could be used here is that of apartheid, as legalized segregation in the South hardly differed from South Africa's policy of total separation of the races to ensure white dominance. In South Africa there was a successful struggle to eliminate apartheid and this should illuminate a similar struggle in Montgomery.

For instance, this quote from Jo Anne Gibson Robinson's

book gives a snapshot of what African Americans went through on the buses in Montgomery before the boycott:

> Black riders would often forget pride and feeling, forget the terribly offensive names they were so often called when they dared to sit in one of the ten reserved seats. Hurting feet, tired bodies, empty stomachs often tempted them to sit down. Names like "black nigger," "black bitches," "heifers," "whores," and so on, brought them to their feet again. When sheer exhaustion or tired, aching limbs forced them to forget pride and feeling, they sat down, sometimes for one minute, maybe two. Even a minute's rest helped some. But they would rise again, either in tears, or retaliating curses hurled at them at the driver. Whatever the case was, they would be badly shaken, nervous, tired, fearful, and angry.
>
> (Jo Anne Gibson Robinson, *The Montgomery Bus Boycott and the Women Who Started It: The Memoir of Jo Anne Gibson Robinson* [Knoxville: University of Tennessee Press, 1987])

I've raised the question of how to expose children to the reality of segregation and racism with a number of educators, both African American and European American. Most of the European American and a few of the African American educators felt that young children do not need to be exposed to the harsh and violent history of segregation in the United States. They worried about the affect such exposure would have on race relations in their classrooms and especially about provoking rage on the part of African American students. The others felt that, given the resurgence of overt racism in the United States these days, allowing rage and anger to come out was the only way African American and European American children could work from the reality of difference and separation toward a common life. They felt that conflict was a positive thing that could be healing when confronted directly, and that avoiding the horrors of racism was just another way of perpetuating them. I agree with this second group and believe that some recasting of the third and fourth sentences of "Rosa Was Tired" is called for:

Those days Alabama was legally segregated. That means that African American people were prevented by the state law from using the same swimming pools, schools, and other public facilities as European Americans. There were also separate entrances, toilets, and drinking fountains for African Americans and European Americans in places such as bus and train stations. Hotels, restaurants, movie theaters, and sports events were also segregated. If an African American violated any of these laws, she or he might be arrested by police or physically attacked by European Americans.

The facilities African Americans were allowed to use were not only separate from the ones European Americans used, but they were also inferior. The reason for this was racism, the belief that European Americans were superior to African Americans and that therefore European Americans deserved better facilities.

> 3. *Whenever it was crowded on the city buses, African Americans had to give up seats in front to European Americans and move to the back of the bus.*

Actually, African Americans were never allowed to sit in the front of the bus in the South in those days. The front seats were *reserved* for European Americans. Between five and ten rows back the "Colored" section began. When the front of the bus filled up, African Americans seated in the "Colored" section had to give up their seats and move toward the back of the bus. Thus, for example, an elderly African American woman would have to give up her seat to a European American teenaged male at the peril of being arrested. Consistent with the comments I've been making so far, and with the truth of the experience of segregation, this sentence should be expanded as follows:

> Those days public buses were divided into two sections, one at the front for European Americans that was supposed to be "for whites only." From five to ten rows back the section for African Americans began. That part of the bus was called the "Colored" section.
>
> Whenever it was crowded on the city buses, African American people were forced to give up seats in the "Colored" section to European Americans and move to the back of the bus. For example, an elderly African American woman would have to give up her seat to a European American teenaged male. If she refused, she could be arrested for breaking the segregation laws.

⌒

4. One day on her way home from work, Rosa was tired and sat down in the front of the bus.

Rosa Parks did not sit in the front of the bus. She sat in the front row of the "Colored" section. When the bus got crowded, she refused to give up her seat in the "Colored" section to a European American. This was not the first time she had refused to move. When she was asked subsequently by Myles Horton, the education director of Highlander Center and its founder, "Mrs. Parks, have you ever moved before?" her response was, "I hadn't for quite a long while." It is important to point this out, as it indicates quite clearly that it was not her intent, on that day, to break the segregation laws since she had been resisting the laws for "quite a long while."

At this point the story lapses into the familiar and refers to Rosa Parks as "Rosa." The question of whether to use the first name for historical characters in a factual story is complicated. One argument in favor of doing so is that young children will more readily identify with characters who are presented in a personalized and familiar way. However, it was a sanctioned social practice in the South during the time of the story for European Americans to call African American adults by their first names as a way of reinforcing their inferior status. African Americans could never call European Americans by their first names without breaking the social code of segregation. It seems unwise, therefore, to use that practice in the story.

In addition, it's reasonable to assume that Rosa Parks was not any more tired on that one day than on other days. She worked at an exhausting full-time job and was also fully active in the community. To emphasize her being tired is another way of saying that her defiance of segregation was an accidental result of her fatigue and consequent short temper on that particular day. Rage, however, is not a one-day thing, and Rosa Parks acted with full knowledge of what she was doing. It is therefore more respectful and historically accurate to make these changes: "December 1, 1955, on her way home from work, Rosa Parks took the bus as usual. She sat down in the front row of the 'Colored' section."

5. *As the bus got crowded she was asked to give up her seat to a European American man, and she refused. The bus driver told her she had to go to the back of the bus, and she still refused to move. It was a hot day, and she was tired and angry and became very stubborn. The driver called a policeman who arrested Rosa.*

Rosa Parks described her experiences with buses in these words:

I had problems with bus drivers over the years because I didn't see fit to pay my money into the front and then go around to the back. Sometimes bus drivers wouldn't permit me to get on the bus, and I had been evicted from the bus. But, as I say, there had been incidents over the years. One of the things that made this . . . (incident) . . . get so much publicity was the fact that the police were called in and I was placed under arrest. See, if I had just been evicted from the bus and he hadn't placed me under arrest or had any charges brought against me, it probably could have been just another incident. (Maria Fleming, ed., *A Place at the Table: Struggles for Equality* [New York: Oxford University Press, 2001], p. 31)

More recently, she described her thoughts that day in the following way:

Having to take a certain section [on a bus] because of your race was humiliating, but having to stand up because a particular driver wanted to keep a white person from having to stand was, to my mind, most inhumane.

More than seventy-five, between eighty-five and I think ninety, percent of the patronage of the buses were black people, because more white people could own and drive their own cars than blacks. I happened to be the secretary of the Montgomery branch of the NAACP as well as the NAACP Youth Council adviser. Many cases did come to my attention that nothing came out of because the person that was abused would be too intimidated to sign an affidavit, or to make a statement. Over the years, I had had my own problems with the bus drivers. In fact, some did tell me not to ride their buses if I felt that I was too important to go to the back door to get on. One had evicted me from the bus in 1943, which did not cause anything more than just a passing glance.

On December 1, 1955, I had finished my day's work as a tailor's assistant in the Montgomery Fair department store and I was on my way home. There was one vacant seat on the Cleveland Avenue bus, which I took, alongside a man and two women across the aisle. There were still a few vacant seats in the white section in the front, of course. We went to the next stop without being disturbed. On the third, the front seats were occupied and this one man, a white man, was standing. The driver asked us to stand up and let him have those seats, and when none of us moved at his first words, he said, "You all make it light on yourselves and let me have those seats." And the man who was sitting next to the window stood up, and I made room for him to pass by me. The two women across the aisle stood up and moved out. When the driver saw me still sitting, he asked if I was going to stand up and I said, "No, I'm not."

And he said, "Well, if you don't stand up, I'm going to call the police and have you arrested."

I said, "You may do that."

He did get off the bus, and I still stayed where I was. Two policemen came on the bus. One of the policemen asked me if the bus driver had asked me to stand and I said yes.

He said, "Why don't you stand up?"

And I asked him, "Why do you push us around?"

He said, "I do not know, but the law is the law and you're under arrest."

> (Henry Hampton and Steve Fayer, *Voices of Freedom*
> [New York: Bantam, 1990], pp. 19, 20)

Mere anger and stubbornness could not account for the clear resolve with which Rosa Parks acted. She knew what she was doing, understood the consequences, and was prepared to confront segregation head-on with whatever sacrifice she had to make. A more accurate account of the event, taking Rosa Parks's past history into consideration, might be:

> As the bus got crowded, the driver demanded that she give up her seat to a European American man and move to the back of the bus. This was not the first time this had happened to Rosa Parks. In the past she refused to move, and the driver simply put her off the bus.
>
> Mrs. Parks hated segregation and, along with many other African American people, refused to obey many of its unfair rules. She refused to do what the bus driver demanded.
>
> The bus driver commanded her once more to go to the back of the bus and she stayed in her seat, looking straight ahead and not moving an inch. He got angry at her and became very stubborn. He called a policeman who arrested Mrs. Parks.

6. *When other African Americans in Montgomery heard this, they became angry too. So they decided to refuse to ride the buses until everyone was allowed to ride together. They boycotted the buses.*

The connection between Rosa Parks's arrest and the boycott is a mystery in most accounts of what happened in Montgomery. Community support for the boycott is portrayed as being instantaneous and miraculously effective the very day after Mrs. Parks was arrested. Things don't happen that way, and it is an insult to the intelligence and courage of the African American community in Montgomery to turn their planned resistance to segregation into a spontaneous emotional response. The actual situation was more interesting and complex. Rosa Parks was not the only person who had defied the bus segregation laws in the past. According to E.D. Nixon, in the three months preceding Mrs. Parks's arrest, at least three other African American people had been arrested in Montgomery for refusing to give up their seats to European American people. In each case, Nixon, a community leader and union activist, along with other people in leadership positions in the African American community in Montgomery investigated the background of the person arrested. They were looking for someone who had the respect of the community and the strength to deal with the racist police force as well as all of the publicity that would result from being at the center of a bus boycott.

In a 1977 interview published in Howell Raines's book *My Soul Is Rested*, Nixon describes the situation in Montgomery:

I'm an old man now, but I'm so proud that I had a part in what happened here in Montgomery. . . .

I'm from Montgomery, Alabama, a city that's known as the Cradle of the Confederacy, that had stood still for more than ninety-three years until Rosa L. Parks was arrested and thrown in jail like a common criminal. . . .

First of all, we'd talked about a bus boycott all the year.

We had three other people prior to Mrs. Parks arrested who reported their incidents to us, but you couldn'ta found nobody in Montgomery would agree to have a bus boycott—and I'm not patting myself on the shoulder—unless it was approved by E.D. . . .

Then, on December one, Rosa L. Parks was arrested. When she was arrested, a friend of hers called my wife and told my wife they'd arrested Mrs. Parks and Mrs. Nixon called my office. . . . She said, "Arrested Mrs. Parks," and I said, "For what?" She said, "I don't know. Go get her," just like I could go get her. I called down there and asked them what was the charge against her, and the desk sergeant said to me, he said, "None of your so-and-so business." Of course, no use of me arguing with him, so I called a white lawyer. Our black lawyer was out of the state at the time, Fred Gray. I called a white lawyer by the name of Clifford J. Durr. I said, "Mr. Durr, they arrested Mrs. Parks." He said, "For what?" and I said, "Something about on the bus. What I want you to do is to call up down there and find out the charges against her." So he called up down there, in a few minutes called me back and said, "The charge is violating the Alabama segregation law."

This leads to the most important point left out in Nixon's interview and in popularized accounts of the Montgomery bus boycott: the boycott had been planned and organized before Rosa Parks was arrested. It was an event waiting to happen, and that is why it could be mobilized so quickly. Rosa Parks's arrest brought it about because she was part of the African

American leadership in Montgomery and was trusted not to cave in under the pressure everyone knew she would be exposed to, including threats to her life.

But the story goes back even farther than that to an African American women's organization in Montgomery called the Woman's Political Council (WPC). The WPC was headed in those days by Jo Ann Gibson Robinson, a professor of English at Alabama State University in Montgomery, an all African American university. In 1949, Robinson was put off a bus in Montgomery for refusing to move to the back of the bus. She and other women in Montgomery resolved to do something about bus segregation.

In her book *The Montgomery Bus Boycott and the Women Who Started It*, Robinson describes her experiences with the buses in Montgomery and her determination as early as 1949 to organize a boycott:

> I was as happy as I had ever been in my life that Saturday morning before Christmas in December 1949 as I prepared to leave the campus of Alabama State College in Montgomery for the holidays. I had been a member of the English faculty at the college since September of that year, and I had loved every minute of it. . . .
>
> I boarded an almost empty city bus, dropped my coins into the proper place, and observed the passengers aboard, only two—a white woman who sat in the third row from the front, and a black man in a seat near the back. I took the fifth row seat from the front and sat down, immediately closing my eyes and envisioning, in my mind's eye,

the wonderful two weeks' vacation I would have with my family and friends in Ohio.

From the far distance of my reverie I thought I heard a voice, an unpleasant voice, but I was too happy to worry about voices, or any noise for that matter. But the same words were repeated, in a stronger, unsavory tone, and I opened my eyes. Immediately I sat up in that seat. The bus driver had stopped the bus, turned in his seat, and was speaking to me!

"If you can sit in the fifth row from the front of the other buses in Montgomery, suppose you get off and ride in one of them!" I heard him, but the message did not register with me. My thoughts were elsewhere. I had not even noticed that the bus had come to a full stop, or I had subconsciously surmised that passengers were getting on or off.

Suddenly the driver left his seat and stood over me. His hand was drawn back as if he were going to strike me. "Get up from there!" he yelled. He repeated it, for, dazed, I had not moved. "Get up from there!"

I leaped to my feet, afraid he would hit me, and ran to the front door to get off the bus. I even stepped down to the lower level, so that when the door was opened, I could step off the bus and hide myself, for tears were falling rapidly from my eyes. It suddenly occurred to me that I was supposed to go to the back door to get off, not the front! However, I was too upset, frightened, and tearful to move. I never could have walked to the rear door. . . .

Even now, when segregation has been abolished and

riders sit where they please on public transportation lines, memories like mine will not fade away. Although almost thirty years have gone by, black people have not forgotten the years leading up to the boycott of 1955.

(Jo Anne Gibson Robinson, *The Montgomery Bus Boycott and the Women Who Started It* [Knoxville: University of Tennessee Press, 1987], p. 17)

Just to emphasize this preparation, Jo Ann Robinson made the following statement:

In 1953, the members of the Women's Political Council (WPC) were confronted with some thirty complaints against the bus company, brought to it by black people in the community. . . .

In Montgomery in 1955, no one was brazen enough to announce publicly that black people might boycott city buses for the specific purpose of integrating those buses. Just to say that minorities wanted "better seating arrangements" was bad enough. That was the term the two sides, white and black, always used later in discussing the boycott. The word "integration" never came up. Certainly all blacks knew not to use that word while riding the bus. To admit that black Americans were seeking to integrate would have been too much; there probably would have been much bloodshed and arrests of those who dared to disclose such an idea! . . .

The WPC, however, knew all the time that black Americans were working for integration, pure and simple.

No front toward back, or vice versa! We knew we were human beings; that neither whites nor blacks were responsible for their color; that someday those buses, of necessity, had to be integrated; and that after integration neither would be worse off. . . . We were, then, bent on integration. There were those afraid to admit it. But, we knew that deep down in the secret minds of all—teachers, students, and community—black Americans wanted integration. That way we would achieve equality. The only way.

This story of collective decision making, willed risk, and coordinated action is more dramatic than the story of an angry individual who sparked a demonstration; it has more to teach children who themselves may have to organize and act collectively against oppressive forces in the future. Here's one way to tell this complex story to young children:

Mrs. Parks was not the first African American person to be arrested in Montgomery for refusing to move to the back of the bus. In the months before her refusal, at least three other people were arrested for the same reason. In fact, African American leaders in Montgomery were planning to overcome segregation. One way they wanted to do this was to have every African American person boycott the buses. Since most of the bus riders in the city were African American, the buses would go broke if they refused to let African Americans and European Americans ride the buses as equals.

From 1949 right up to the day Mrs. Parks refused to move, the Woman's Political Council of Montgomery prepared to stage a bus boycott because of how African Americans were treated on the bus. African American people in Montgomery were ready to support the boycott. They were just waiting for the right time. Nineteen fifty-five was the time.

However, none of the people who were arrested before Mrs. Parks was a leader. She was, and the day she was arrested the leadership called a meeting at the Dexter Avenue Baptist Church. They decided to begin their refusal to ride the buses the next morning. They knew Mrs. Parks had the courage to deal with the pressure of defying segregation and would not yield even if her life was threatened.

The next day the Montgomery bus boycott began.

7. *The boycott, which was led by Martin Luther King Jr., succeeded. Now African Americans and European Americans can ride the buses together in Montgomery. Rosa Parks was a very brave person.*

The Montgomery bus boycott was planned by the WPC, E.D. Nixon, and others, and led by Marin Luther King Jr., who was chosen to be the public face of the boycott because of his charisma and moral integrity.

Jo Anne Gibson Robinson describes the specific strategy for informing the community about the boycott in the following way:

[T]he WPC officers previously had discussed plans for distributing thousands of notices announcing a bus boycott. Now the time had come for me to write just such a notice. I sat down and quickly drafted a message and then called a colleague, who had access to the college's mimeograph equipment. When I told him that the WPC was staging a boycott and needed to run off the notices, he told me that he too had suffered embarrassment on the city buses. Like myself, he had been hurt and angry. He said that he would happily assist me. . . . By 4:00 A.M. Friday, the sheets had been duplicated, cut in thirds, and bundled. Each leaflet read:

Another Negro woman has been arrested and thrown in jail because she refused to get up out of her seat on the bus for a white person to sit down. It is the second time since the Claudette Colvin case that a Negro woman has been arrested for the same thing. This has to be stopped. Negroes have rights, too, for if Negroes did not ride the buses, they could not operate. Three-fourths of the riders are Negroes, yet we are arrested, or have to stand over empty seats.

If we do not do something to stop these arrests, they will continue.

The next time it may be you, or your daughter, or mother. This woman's case will come up on Monday. We are, therefore, asking every Negro to stay off the buses Monday in protest of the arrest and trial. Don't ride the buses to work, to town, to school.

At the time of the boycott, Martin Luther King Jr. was a new member of the community. He had just taken over the Dexter Avenue Baptist Church, and when Nixon told him that Rosa Parks's arrest was just what everybody was waiting for to kick off a bus boycott and assault the institution of segregation, King was at first reluctant. However, the community leaders chose him, and he accepted their call. They were ready and organized, and King had both the contacts in Atlanta and the charisma to take a leading role. E.D. Nixon describes King's involvement in this interview, published in Howell Raines's *My Soul Is Rested*:

I had almost a life history of being rebellious against being mistreated because of my color, and although no one could have predicted that moment on the bus, Rosa Parks's "life history" had prepared her for it. . . . And so after we agreed [on the boycott], oh, I guess we spent a couple of hours discussing this thing. Then I went home and I took a sheet of paper and I drew right in the center of the paper. I used that for the square and then I used Hunter Station, Washington Park, Pickett Springs, all the different areas in Montgomery, and I used a slide rule to get a estimate. I discovered nowhere in Montgomery at that time a man couldn't walk to work if he wanted to. I said, "We can beat this thing." . . .

So anyhow. I recorded quite a few names, starting off with Rev. Abernathy, Rev. Hubbard, Rev. King, and on down the line, and I called some of the people who represent peoples so that they could get the word out. The first man I

During the boycott many people walked to work no matter what the weather or the distance they had to go. (Time and Life Pictures/Getty Images)

called was Reverend Ralph Abernathy. He said, "Yes, Brother Nixon, I'll go along. I think it's a good thing."

The second person I called was the late Reverend H.H. Hubbard. He said, "Yes, I'll go along with you."

And I called Rev. King, was number three, and he said, "Brother Nixon, let me think about it awhile, and call me back."

When I called him back, he was number nineteen, and of course, he agreed to go along. I said, "I'm glad you agreed because I already set the meeting up to meet at your church." . . .

Mrs. Parks was tried that morning and she was found guilty. . . . I'd been in court off and on for twenty years, hearing different peoples, and very seldom, if ever, there was another black man unless he was being tried. But that particular morning, the morning of December the fifth, 1955, the black man was reborn again. I couldn't believe it when they found her guilty and I had to go through the vestibule down the hall to the clerk's office to sign her appeal bond. . . . People came in that other door, and that door was about ten feet wide, and they was just that crowded in there, people wanting to know what happened. I said, "Well, they found her guilty. Now, I'm gon' have to make another bond for her. As soon as we can get her bond signed, we'll bring her right out." They said, "If you don't hurry and come out, we're coming in there and getchya." I couldn't believe it. When we got outside, police were standing outside with sawed-off shotguns, and the people all up and down the streets was from sidewalk to side-walk out there. I looked around there, and I bet you there was over a thousand black people—black men—on the streets out there.

I know if they'da found her not guilty, we'da had the same thing again. They really did the thing that was best for us when they found her guilty. . . .

[Nixon made several] recommendations. . . . I know one was "Seating on the bus, first come, first served," and "Negro bus drivers in predominant Negro neighborhoods," and "More courtesy to Negro patrons."

At that point, members of the community created the Montgomery Improvement Association and had to choose a leader. Nixon discusses the process:

He said, "Brother Nixon, now you gon' serve as president, ain'tchya?" I said, "Naw, not unless'n you all don't accept my man." He said, "Who is your man?" I said, "Martin Luther King." He said, "I'll go along with it." French said, "I'll go along with it." So then we had not only our recommendation, our resolution, our name, we had our president.

In August of 1955 he was the guest speaker for the NAACP, and a professor over at the State Teachers College and I were sitting in the back. His name was J.E. Pierce. When King got through talking, I said, "Pierce, you know that guy made a heck of a speech."

He said, "I agree with you. He sho' did."

I said, "I don't know how I'm going to do it yet, but someday I'm gon' hang him to the stars."

King accepted his role; and Nixon responded to King's speech at the Montgomery Improvement Association's first rally:

Rev. King made a masterpiece that evenin'. So when he did, then I came behind him, and I never shall forget, I said, "Good evenin', my friends." I said, "I'm so happy to see all of you out here tonight, but I wanna tell you somethin'. If you're scared, you better get your hat and coat and go home. It's gon' be a long drawn-out affair and before it's over with somebody gon' die." I said, "May be me, I don't know. . . . The only request I have is if I'm the one that dies, don't let me die in vain. For twenty-some-odd years I been fighting and saying to myself that I didn't want the children to come along and have to suffer all the insults that I've suffered. Well, hell, I changed my mind tonight." Just like that. "I decided that I wanted to enjoy some of this freedom myself." And everybody hollered when I said that.

The boycott lasted 381 inconvenient days, something not usually mentioned in children's books. It did succeed, and it was one of the events that sparked the entire Civil Rights Movement. People who had been planning an overt attack on segregation for years took that victory as a sign that the time was ripe, even though the people involved in the Montgomery

Rosa Parks getting back on the bus after the boycott was ended and the buses desegregated. (Time and Life Pictures/Getty Images)

bus boycott did not themselves anticipate such results. Here's one possible way to convey this to children:

> There was a young new minister in Montgomery, those days. His name was Martin Luther King Jr. People in the community felt that he was a special person and asked him to lead the boycott. At first he wasn't sure. He worried about the violence that might result from the boycott. However, he quickly made up his mind that it was time to destroy segregation and accepted the people's call for him to be their leader.
>
> The Montgomery bus boycott lasted 381 days. For over a year the African American people of Montgomery, Alabama, stayed off the buses. Some walked to work, others rode bicycles or shared car rides. It was very hard for them, but they knew that what they were doing was very important for all African American people in the South.
>
> The boycott succeeded, and by the end of 1956, African Americans and European Americans could ride the buses in Montgomery as equals.
>
> However, the struggle for the complete elimination of segregation had just begun.
>
> We all owe a great deal to the courage and intelligence of Rosa Parks and the entire African American community of Montgomery, Alabama. They took risks to make democracy work for all of us.

Following is the complete text of the reconstructed story of Rosa Parks and the Montgomery bus boycott. The language is simple, but the story is complex, and it deserves to be told with appropriate complexity rather than simplified or rendered innocuous by trivializing the events of 1955. Children can work through hard and painful questions of history, psychology, and culture if they are guided by a caring adult and provided with materials that challenge them.

She Would Not Be Moved: The Story of Rosa Parks and the Montgomery Bus Boycott

It was 1955. Everyone in the African American community in Montgomery, Alabama, knew Rosa Parks. She was a community leader, and people admired her courage. All throughout her life she had opposed prejudice, even if it got her into trouble with European American people.

Those days Alabama was legally segregated. That means that African American people were prevented by the state law from using the same swimming pools, schools, and other public facilities as European Americans. There also were separate entrances, toilets, and drinking fountains for African Americans and European Americans in places such as bus and train stations. Hotels, restaurants, movie theaters, and sports events were also segregated. If an African American violated any of these laws she or he might be arrested by police or physically attacked by European Americans.

The facilities African Americans were allowed to use were not only separate from the ones European Americans

Rosa Parks received the Congressional Gold Medal of Honor in 1999. It is the highest honor a civilian can receive in the United States. (Time and Life Pictures/Getty Images)

used, but they were also inferior. The reason for this was racism, the belief that European Americans were superior to African Americans and that therefore European Americans deserved better facilities.

Those days public buses were divided into two sections. The section at the front was for European Americans. It was supposed to be "for whites only." From five to ten rows back, the section for African Americans began. That part of the bus was called the "Colored" section.

Whenever it was crowded on the city buses, African American people were forced to give up seats in the "Colored" section to European Americans and move to the back of the bus. For example, an elderly African American woman would have to give up her seat to a European American teenaged male. If she refused she could be arrested for breaking the segregation laws.

On December 1, 1955, Rosa Parks took the bus on her way home from work as usual. She sat down in the front row of the "Colored" section. As the bus got crowded, the driver demanded that she give up her seat to a European American man, and move to the back of the bus. This was not the first time this had happened to Rosa Parks. In the past she refused to move, and the driver simply put her off the bus. Mrs. Parks hated segregation, and along with many other African American people, she refused to obey many of its unfair rules. She refused to do what the bus driver demanded.

The bus driver, who was European American, commanded her once more to go to the back of the bus and she stayed in her seat, looking straight ahead and not moving an inch. It was a hot day, and the driver was angry and became very stubborn. He called a policeman, who arrested Mrs. Parks.

Mrs. Parks was not the first African American person to be arrested in Montgomery for refusing to move to the back of the bus. In the months before her refusal, at least three other people were arrested for the same reason. In fact, African American leaders in Montgomery were planning to overcome segregation. One way they wanted to do this was to have every African American person boycott the buses. Since most of the bus riders in the city were African American, the buses would go broke if they refused to let African Americans and European Americans ride the buses as equals.

From 1949 right up to the day Mrs. Parks refused to move, the Woman's Political Council of Montgomery prepared to stage a bus boycott because of how African Americans were treated on the bus. They were just waiting for the right time. Nineteen fifty-five was that time.

However, none of the people who were arrested before Mrs. Parks, was a leader. She was, and the day she was arrested, the leadership called a meeting at the Dexter Avenue Baptist Church. They decided to begin their refusal to ride the buses the next morning. They knew Mrs. Parks had the courage to deal with the pressure of defying segregation and would not yield, even if her life was threatened.

The next day the Montgomery bus boycott began.

There was a young new minister in Montgomery in those days. His name was Martin Luther King Jr. People in the community felt that he was a special person and asked him to lead the boycott. At first he wasn't sure. He worried about the violence that might result from the boycott. However, he quickly made up his mind that it was time to destroy segregation and accepted the people's call for him to be their leader.

The Montgomery bus boycott lasted 381 days. For over a year the African American people of Montgomery, Alabama, stayed off the buses. Some walked to work, others rode bicycles, or shared car rides. It was very inconvenient for them, but they knew that what they were doing was very important for all African American people in the South.

The boycott succeeded, and by the end of 1956, African American and European American people could ride the buses in Montgomery as equals. However, the struggle for the complete elimination of segregation had just begun.

We all owe a great deal to the courage and intelligence of Rosa Parks and the entire African American community of Montgomery, Alabama. They took risks to try to make democracy work for all of us.

Concluding Thoughts

The revised version of the bus boycott story is about Rosa
Parks, but it is also about the African American people of
Montgomery, Alabama. It takes the usual, individualized version of the Rosa Parks tale and puts it in the context of a coher-
ent, community-based social struggle. This does not diminish
Rosa Parks in any way. It places her, however, in the midst of a
consciously planned movement for social change and reminds
me of the freedom song "We Shall Not Be Moved," for it was
precisely Rosa Parks's and the community's refusal to be moved
that made the boycott possible.

As it turns out, my retelling of the story of Rosa Parks and
the Montgomery bus boycott is certainly not the only one. In
2005, fifty years after the event, some new, moving, and historically accurate books about the events in Montgomery have
been published. One, for example, is *Rosa Parks: The Movement
Organizes* (Englewood, NJ: Silver Burdett, 1990) by Kai
Friese, which is one of nine volumes in a series edited by the
scholar Eldon Morris titled *The History of the Civil Rights Movement*. Other volumes in the series, such as those about Ella
Baker and Fannie Lou Hamer, also provide a fuller, more accurate look at people's struggles during the Civil Rights Movement of the 1960s than has been available to young people
until now.

These volumes are gifts to all of us from a number of African
American scholars who have reclaimed history from the distor-
tions and omissions of years of irresponsible writing for children about the Civil Rights Movement. They are models of

how history and biography can directly confront racial conflicts and illuminate social struggles. This is particularly true of the Rosa Parks volume, which brings the reader up-to-date in Mrs. Parks's life and informs us that she remained active over the years, working for social and economic justice in Congressman John Conyers's office in Detroit, Michigan. The book, which credits all of the people involved in making the Montgomery bus boycott possible, provides a portrait of a community mobilized for justice. It also leaves us with a sense of the ongoing struggle to eliminate racism in the United States.

Some of the more recent books have begun to tell the story in a more historically responsible way, especially with the publication of Rosa Parks's autobiography. The current change in awareness of Rosa Parks's story is explicitly recognized in the following biographical entry from the *Cambridge Dictionary of American Biography*:

Parks, Rosa (1913–) civil rights activist; born in Tuskegee, Ala. After briefly attending Alabama State University, she married and settled in Montgomery, Ala., where she worked as a tailor's assistant in a department store. Contrary to most early portrayals of her as merely a poor seamstress, who on the spur of a moment refused to surrender her seat in a bus to a white person, she had long been a community activist—she had served as the secretary of the National Association for the Advancement of Colored People and she worked for the Union of Sleeping Car Porters. She had also been involved in previous incidents when refusing to leave a bus seat. By forcing the police to remove, arrest, and imprison her on this occasion, and then agreeing to become a test case of segregation ordinances, she played a deliberate role in instigating the Montgomery bus boycott (1955–56). She was fired from her job at the department store and in 1957 she became a youth worker in Detroit, Michigan. As she eventually earned recognition as the "midwife" or "mother" of the civil rights revolution, she became a sought-after speaker nationally.

> (John S. Bowman, ed., *Cambridge Dictionary of American Biography* [New York: Cambridge University Press, 1995], p. 558)

In addition, a new book aimed at a school audience and authored by Pulitzer Prize winner Diane McWorther, *A Dream of Freedom*, introduces Rosa Parks and her role in the Montgomery bus boycott in the following way:

> It was dark by 5:30 P.M. on December 1, 1955. The Christmas lights had been turned on in Montgomery, the capital of Alabama. A forty-two-year-old black seamstress left her $23-dollar-a-week tailoring job at a downtown department store. She boarded a bus for home. After a few stops the bus was full. A white man was left standing. . . .
>
> Three black passengers obeyed. The fourth sitting with them, the seamstress, defiantly slid over to the window and refused to move to the back of the bus. The black struggle for freedom had found the route into its future.
>
> That seamstress was Rosa Parks. In the legends that grew up around her, she came to be seen as a sweet, simple

woman with tired feet who decided one day that she would not be moved. But Parks had been in training for this moment all her life. And the "tired" she felt was the kind of fatigue of the soul that has built for decades and finally sets off a revolution.

(Diane McWorther, *A Dream of Freedom* [New York: Scholastic Nonfiction, 2004], pp. 40–41)

Would that the school texts and the most common young people's books available in schools were as honest and clear about Rosa Parks as these distinguished books. However, that is not the case. For example, *The Montgomery Bus Boycott* by Frank Walsh describes Rosa Parks's action in the following way:

On the evening of December 1, 1955, a tailor's assistant named Rosa Parks left her job at a Montgomery department store and waited at a bus stop for a ride home. Parks had experienced the humiliation of inequity and racism on the buses before. In fact, when she boarded the bus that night, she recognized the driver, James Blake. On a rainy night some twelve years before, Blake had ordered Parks to get on his bus using the rear entrance. When Parks stepped off the bus to come in through the back door, Blake had driven away, leaving her to walk home in the rain.

The night in December 1955, however, Parks did get on board. The bus was already crowded, and at the next stop even more passengers boarded. The driver ordered the blacks who were sitting to give up their seats for the white riders. Although she had not planned to do so, Rosa

Parks refused to move. Blake threatened to call the police and have Parks arrested. Parks replied, "You may do that."
    (Frank Walsh, *The Montgomery Bus Boycott*
    [Milwaukee, WI: World Almanac Library, 2003])

The author fails to mention that Mrs. Parks had long since refused to move to the back of the bus. It's just that she had never been arrested before. To his credit, however, the author does show Rosa Parks's dignity and resolve by quoting her remark, "You may do that."

Finally, and most important, Rosa Parks has written an autobiography that presents a more personal version of the story given here and shows her continuing commitment to social justice. In the book she talks about her childhood in the South and her early confrontations with racism. I heartily recommend this book for anyone who wants a complex picture of Rosa Parks's formative years and of the values she fought for in Montgomery and throughout her life.

The following gives us a hint of how she feels now that she is in her nineties:

All those laws against segregation have been passed, and all that progress has been made. But a whole lot of white people's hearts have not been changed. Dr. King used to talk about the fact that if a law was changed, it might not change hearts but it would offer some protection. He was right. We now have some protection, but there is still much racism and racial violence. . . .

Sometimes I do feel pretty sad about some of the events

that have taken place recently. I try to keep hope alive anyway, but that's not always the easiest thing to do. I have spent over half my life teaching love and brotherhood, and I feel that it is better to continue to try to teach or live equality and love than it would be to have hatred or prejudice. Everyone living together in peace and harmony and love that's the goal that we seek, and I think that the more people there are who reach that state of mind, the better we will all be.

(Rosa Parks, with Jim Haskins, *Rosa Parks, My Story*
[Puffin Books, 2002])

Once again Rosa Parks, the humane activist, is challenging us today to do more than just memorialize the past but to act in the present and in the future. However, when the story of the Montgomery bus boycott is told merely as a tale of a single heroic person, it leaves children hanging or searching for someone to follow, when *they* should be the actors. Not everyone is a hero or heroine. Of course, the idea that only special people can create change is useful if you want to prevent mass movements and keep change from happening. Not every child can be Rosa Parks, but everyone can imagine her- or himself as a participant in the boycott. As a tale of a social movement and a community effort to overthrow injustice, the Rosa Parks story, as I've tried to retell it, creates the possibility of every child identifying her- or himself as an activist, as someone who can help make justice happen. And it is that kind of empowerment that people in the United States desperately need at this low and demoralized time in our history.

Appendix

The following quotes are taken from children's books and school textbooks. Almost all illustrate the myth of Rosa Parks, the Tired. The earliest publication date is 1976, and the rest were published in their current form in the 1980s and 1990s. Two of the children's books, however, were copyrighted in 1969 and reissued in the 1980s with new illustrations. No attempt was made in these two works to update the material, and they are still used in many schools, usually without any supplementary material that would provide a more developed view of Rosa Parks or of the boycott.

The sample included is representative of dozens I've read and cumulatively represents all of the different aspects of the Rosa Parks myth I portrayed in "Rosa Was Tired." Some of the other texts and the specific lines that relate to my text are listed at the end of this appendix. The passages quoted more fully here are from the most progressive texts and trade books that I've found. I have avoided citing texts that are no longer in print. Finally, I've added some newer texts that represent a fuller portrait of the role Rosa Parks and other members of the Montgomery community played in developing and sustaining the boycott and eventually desegregating the buses in

Montgomery. These texts supplement texts already mentioned in this chapter.

1. This excerpt is from Valerie Schloredt, *Martin Luther King Jr: America's Great Nonviolent Leader in the Struggle for Human Rights* (Harrisburg, PA: Morehouse Publishing, 1990), pp. 19, 20.

On the evening of Dec. 1, 1955, a black lady named Rosa Parks left the downtown department store where she worked as a seamstress and walked to the bus stop to catch the bus that would take her home.

The book goes on to describe what happened when Mrs. Parks refused to move to the back of the bus: "Mrs. Parks was tired. She had a long, hard day. . . . Something snapped in Mrs. Parks at that moment. Perhaps the patience with which she had endured years of subservience and insult . . . Mrs. Parks didn't look like a person to challenge the law of Montgomery. She was a quiet looking lady, wearing small steel-rimmed spectacles; but like thousands of other black people who rode the buses day after day, she was weary of being treated with such contempt.

Much later she was asked if she had planned her protest. "No," she answered. "I was just plain tired, and my feet hurt."

Mrs. Parks's patience had given way, had she but known it, at the best possible moment.

I have not been able to find any source for the quote about Rosa Parks's feet hurting.

2. Here is the Random House version for first to third graders from James T. Kay, *Meet Martin Luther King Jr.* (New York: Step-up Books, Random House, 1969), reprinted with a new cover in 1989.

On Dec. 1, 1955, a woman named Rosa Parks did something about the Jim Crow buses.

Mrs. Parks was black. She worked in a department store. That evening she climbed the bus and sat down.

Each time the bus stopped, more people got on. Soon no seats were left in the white part of the bus.

At the next stop some white people got on. The driver got up and walked over to Mrs. Parks. He told her to give her seat to a white woman.

But Rosa Parks was tired. She did something she had never done before. She just stayed in her seat. . . .

Black people all over the city heard about Rosa Parks. They were very angry. They were mad at the Jim Crow laws. They were mad at the police. They were mad at the bus company. But what could they do?

Then one man said, "Why don't we boycott the buses?" This meant that all the black people would stop riding the buses. Soon the bus company would lose money. Maybe then the owners would be fair to blacks.

3. This selection is from Dharathula H. Millender's work *Martin Luther King Jr.: Young Man with a Dream* (New York: Alladin Books, 1986); *Martin Luther King, Jr.: Boy with a Dream* (Indianapolis: Bobbs Merrill, 1969, pp. 148–9). It is one of the finest of the older children's books about the Civil Rights Movement.

Things came to a head over bus segregation on December 1, 1955. Mrs. Rosa Parks, an attractive Negro seamstress, boarded a bus in downtown Montgomery. This was the same bus she had boarded many times after a hard day's work. Today she was tired and eager to get off her aching feet. Accordingly, she sat down in the first seat in the Negro section behind the section reserved for white passengers.

At first the driver was surprised (when she refused to move) wondering whether he had heard correctly. When Mrs. Parks clung to her seat, however, and held her head proudly in the air, he realized that he was facing trouble. Accordingly, he stopped his bus, called the police, and had her arrested. Her arrest attracted wide attention because she was one of the most respected people in the Negro community. It helped to start a Negro revolt not only in Montgomery but all across the nation.

4. This excerpt is from the upper elementary grade level social studies textbook *The United States and the Other Americas* (New York: Macmillan, 1982), p. 141, by Allan King, Ida Dennis, and Florence Potter, in the Macmillan Social Studies series.

In 1955 Rosa Parks, a black, refused to give up her bus seat to a white in Montgomery, Alabama. She was arrested because of this. Other blacks, led by Dr. Martin Luther King Jr., of Atlanta, Georgia, refused to ride the city buses. The following year a federal court ruled that segregated buses were no longer allowed.

In the teacher's edition (p. 413), the following instructions are given to teachers:

Have the pupils read the rest of page 141. Draw their attention to the photograph of Rosa Parks. Explain that on December 1, 1955, Rosa Parks boarded a bus in Montgomery, Alabama. Her arms were full of groceries, so she sat in the front row of the section of the bus in which blacks were permitted to sit. As the bus filled up, more white people got on, and the bus driver told Rosa to give up her seat to a white person. Rosa looked out the window and pretended not to hear him. She refused to give up her seat, and because of this she was arrested. In protest against her arrest, the black people of Montgomery refused to ride the bus. They formed car pools, walked, rode mules and horses and buggies. On April 23, 1956, the Supreme Court declared that state and local laws that required segregation of buses were unconstitutional.

5. This excerpt is taken from Allan O. Kownslar and William R. Fielder, *Inquiring about American History* (in the Holt Databank System) (New York: Holt, Rinehart and Winston, 1976), p. 301. This is a "modern" series based on inquiry and is considered too liberal for many school districts. It is for upper elementary and junior high school students.

For the black citizens of Montgomery, Alabama, some of the "separate but equal" laws had been changed by

1955. . . . But, in spite of these changes, many people still refused to treat blacks and whites equally. Rosa Parks, a black woman who lived in Montgomery in 1955, had to deal with this problem.

One evening, Rosa Parks was coming home from work on a Montgomery city bus. She had been working hard all day at her job in a downtown department store. Rosa was quite tired. She took a seat toward the back of the bus, where black passengers normally sat. The bus began to fill quickly. As whites got on, they took what seats there were, and soon the bus was full.

Rosa realized that some of the blacks would be asked to give up their seats and move to the back of the bus. They would be asked to stand so that white passengers could sit. She felt that this was unfair. Why should she have to move?

Suddenly the driver turned and asked her, and some other blacks, to move to the rear of the bus. Rosa argued with the driver, but he still insisted that she leave her seat and stand in the back. Rosa paused. She had to make a decision quickly. Should she give up her seat or remain seated?

What would you have done if you had been Rosa Parks? What do you think she did?

Rosa Parks made her choice. She decided to remain seated on the bus. Her action led to the Montgomery Bus Boycott—and eventually, to a Supreme Court ruling against the separation of blacks and whites on all buses.

6. This selection is from another upper elementary grade level text by Timothy Helmus, Val Arnsdorf, Edgar Toppin, and Norman Pounds, *The United States and Its Neighbors* (Morristown, NJ: Silver Burdett, 1984), p. 248.

Dr. King gained nationwide fame in Montgomery, Alabama, in 1955. At that time blacks had to sit in the back of public buses. But one day a quiet woman named Rosa Parks decided to sit in the "whites only" part of the bus. She was arrested. Dr. King led a boycott of Montgomery buses to protest her arrest. People who supported Dr. King would not use the buses until anyone could sit wherever she or he pleased. The boycott worked.

Here is a list of quotes from a sampling of other texts for all grade levels dealing with Rosa Parks and the Montgomery bus boycott. I've quoted from only twenty-four of the dozens of books I consulted, though I think the unity of the story comes across quite clearly. The word "racism" was not used in any of them.

1. Karen McAuley et al., *The United States Past to Present*, Teacher's Edition, Grade 5 (Lexington, MA: D.C. Heath and Company, 1987), p. 405.

It had been a long, hard day and she was tired.

2. Susan Williams McKay, *The World of Mankind*, Grade 3 (Chicago, IL: Follet Publishing Company, 1973), p. 221.

Mrs. Parks sat alone. She was tired. She decided not to move.

3. *The United States: Its History and Neighbors*, Teacher's Edition, Grade 5 (Orlando, FL: Harcourt Brace Jovanovich, 1988), p. 507.

> On Dec. 1, 1955, Rosa Parks sank wearily to her seat on the bus in Montgomery, Alabama.
>
> As the bus filled up, Rosa Parks was asked to give up her seat. She refused. The bus driver called the police, and she was taken to jail.

4. Leonard C. Wood et al., *America: Its People and Values*, Teacher's Edition, Junior High (1985), p. 721.

> On that day a black seamstress named Rosa Parks refused to give up her seat in the white section of the bus.
>
> There as in many other parts of the South, local laws kept public places strictly segregated. Restaurants, businesses, and all forms of public transportation had separate sections for blacks and whites.

5. Kownslar and Fielder, *Inquiring about American History*, Grade 5 (New York: Holt, Rinehart and Winston, 1976), p. 301.

> One evening, Rosa Parks was coming home from work, on a Montgomery city bus. She had been working hard all day at her job. . . . Rosa was quite tired.
>
> Suddenly, the driver turned and asked her, and some other blacks, to move to the rear of the bus. Rosa argued with the driver.

6. JoAnn Cangemi, *Our History*, Grade 5 (New York: Holt, Rinehart, and Winston, 1983), pp. 388–9.

In 1955, a black woman named Rosa Parks sat down in the front of the bus in Montgomery, Alabama. Parks refused to get up from the seat so that a white person could sit down and she was arrested.

Angry about the arrest, Montgomery blacks refused to ride city buses.

The bus boycott was led by Dr. Martin Luther King Jr.

7. Beverly J. Armento et al., *This Is My Country*, Grade 4 (Boston, MA: Houghton Mifflin Company, 1991), p. 98.

She was tired and her feet hurt.

At that time, black and white people, had to sit in separate sections on the bus. Other places were divided too, such as restrooms, waiting rooms, movie theatres and restaurants.

8. Henry F. Graff, *America: The Glorious Republic, Volume 2*, Junior High School and High School (1986), pp. 349–50.

[A] seamstress named Rosa Parks took a courageous and fateful step. . . .

[T]he next day the 50,000 black citizens of Montgomery began a boycott of city buses.

9. *America: The Glorious Republic*, Junior High School and High School (Henry F. Graff, 1985), pp. 717–8.

The next day the 50,000 black citizens of Montgomery began a bus boycott of the city's buses: choosing to walk rather than ride under humiliating conditions.

10. John Edward Wiltz, *The Search for Identity: Modern American History*, Junior High (Philadelphia, PA: J.B. Lippincott Company, 1973), p. 684.

When Mrs. Parks, a small, soft-spoken woman boarded the Cleveland Avenue bus she was tired and her feet hurt.

11. Beverly Jeanne Armento et al., *Living in Our Country*, Grade 5 (River Forest, IL: Laidlaw Brothers Publishing, 1988), pp. 417–8.

In Montgomery, Alabama, a black woman was arrested for using a seat in the front of a bus.
For this reason many black people refused to ride the buses in Montgomery.

12. Glen M. Linden et al., *Legacy of Freedom: A History of the United States*, Junior High School and High School (1986), p. 670.

Tired after a long day's work, Mrs. Parks boarded a bus for home and refused to give up her seat to a white passenger when asked to do so by the bus driver.
The leaders of Montgomery's black community were outraged. Almost at once, they organized a boycott of the Mongomery transit system.

13. Ernest R. May, *A Proud Nation*, Junior High School, Teacher's Edition (Evanston, IL: McDougal, Littell and Company, 1983), p. 691.

On Dec. 1, Rosa Parks, a black woman, refused to give up her seat in the front of a bus to a white person. She had simply worked hard all day, Parks said, and her feet hurt.

14. Alma Graham et al., *United States: Our Nation and Neighbors*, Grade 5 (New York: McGraw Hill), p. 340.

The bus boycott was led by Dr. Martin Luther King Jr.

15. George Vuicich et al., *United States*, Grade 5 (1983), p. 322.

In 1955, a black woman, Rosa Parks, refused to give up her seat on a bus in Montgomery, Alabama. She was arrested. Some people became determined to do something. Blacks in Montgomery began a boycott of the city's buses.

[T]he bus boycott was led by Dr. Martin Luther King Jr.

16. Henry F. Graff et al., *The Promise of Democracy: The Grand Experiment*, Junior High School and High School (Chicago, IL: Rand, McNally and Company, 1978), pp. 365–6.

[I]n many southern communities, black people had to sit at the back of the city buses.

[A]nd she was tired.

17. Dr. Roger M. Berg, Social Studies Series, Grade 5 (Scott Fores-
    man, 1979), p. 335.

    In some cities, blacks were forced to ride in separate
    parts of buses. In 1955, in Montgomery, Alabama, Rosa
    Parks wanted to sit in a part of a public bus set aside for
    whites. She was arrested. The black people of Mont-
    gomery refused to ride the city buses until they could sit
    where they wanted.

18. Richard H. Loftin et al., *Our Country's Communities*, Grade 3
    (Morristown, NJ: Silver, Burdett and Ginn Inc., 1988), p. 246.

    One day a black woman named Rosa Parks got on a
    bus and found the back seats filled. She had been working
    all day and was tired. She sat down in another seat and
    was arrested.
    With Dr. King as their leader, the black people of
    Montgomery refused to ride on the bus until they had the
    same rights as the other riders.
    They did as he [King] said and finally won out.

19. Here is another selection from a much more recent high school
    social studies textbook by Lawrence Broughton, Dr. Dorothy
    Fields, Nadine Liebow, and Paula Young, *United States History*
    (Parsippany, NJ: Pearson Education, 2001), p. 474.

    On December 1, 1995, Rosa Parks, an African Ameri-
    can, got on a bus in Montgomery, Alabama. What she did
    next would lead to huge changes in American society.

Many African Americans and others would take part in nonviolent, or peaceful, protests. They would use these protests to change laws and gain equal rights for all Americans.

Rosa Parks was tired when she got on the bus. She took a seat in the first row of the African American section of the bus. As the bus became more crowded, there were no more seats for white people in the front. The white bus driver ordered Parks to give her seat to a white passenger. She refused. The bus driver called police. Parks was arrested.

20. This extract is from another recent high school social studies textbook by Wayne E. King, *United States History* (Circle Pines, MN: American Guidance Service, 2001), p. 557. It tells the story of the bus boycott and Rosa Parks's development in a much more accurate and respectful way.

In December of 1955, Rosa Parks, a forty-two-year-old African American woman, got on a bus in Montgomery, Alabama. She found a seat near the front. The bus driver asked Parks to give up her seat to a white person. Rosa Parks would not. Police were called and she was arrested. Parks had not planned to challenge the law on that day. She said, "I felt it was just something that I had to do." Her decision not to move from her seat on a bus was the quiet beginning of a national civil rights movement.

In the teacher's edition (p. 557), the following instructions are given to teachers:

Rosa Parks is sometimes described as someone who almost accidentally became a part of the civil rights movement. Actually, she was a college graduate and a political activist. She had been a youth adviser and secretary for the Montgomery NAACP at the Highlander Center, where both African Americans and white Americans were trained to be active participants in the labor movement. She said that when she made her famous protest, she had realized that "all of our meetings, trying to negotiate, bring about petitions before authorities . . . really hadn't done any good at all.

In this case, appropriate information about Rosa Parks is provided to teachers and it is their choice to teach it or not. The students get the old bare bones story.

21. Here is another description from a high school textbook currently in use. Roger LeRoy Miller, *West's American Government* (St. Paul, MN: West Publishing Company, 1994), pp. 144–5.

In 1955, one year after the Brown decision, an African-American woman named Rosa Parks in Montgomery, Alabama, boarded a public bus. When it became crowded, she refused to move to the "colored section" at the rear of the bus. She was arrested and fined for violating Alabama's segregation laws. Her refusal and arrest spurred the local African-American community to organize a year long boycott of the entire Montgomery bus system.

On page 146, the textbook provides this page about Rosa Parks. It is presented as a feature, separate from the text, and is much more relevant to the full story of Rosa Parks and the boycott, though the Highlander connection and the fact that Rosa Parks had often refused to move are left out. It also provides some questions for students to answer that seem to denigrate Rosa Parks's lifelong involvement in the struggle for civil rights. Notice in particular the phrasing of the second question.

Early in December 1955 in Montgomery, Alabama, forty-year-old Rosa Parks boarded the bus to go home from work. The bus was filled, and when a white man boarded, the driver called on the four blacks to move to the back. Three got up and moved, but Parks, tired from a long day of working and the injustice of always having to move for white people, refused to move. She was promptly arrested.

The arrest of Parks ignited a protest that spread spontaneously through the African American community. Several leaders, including the Reverend Martin Luther King Jr., organized a boycott of the city's bus lines. The boycott inspired confidence and pride in the African-American community and a feeling spread that it was time for changes in race relations. Finally, in December 1956, as a result of the Supreme Court's intervention against segregation in public transportation, blacks and whites rode together on unsegregated buses for the first time in Alabama. The courage of

Parks served as catalyst to end segregation of buses, trains, lunch counters, and other public facilities in the South.

Rosa Parks was born on February 4, 1913, in Tuskegee, Alabama. Her childhood was marked by fears of the Ku Klux Klan and their persecution of African Americans. She studied at Alabama State College, worked briefly at clerical jobs, and finally became a tailor's assistant at a department store. Her husband, Raymond Parks, was a barber. The only indicator of her involvement in civil rights was her volunteer work for the NAACP, in which she helped campaign to register African American voters.

Although Parks's action and arrest began civil rights activism in Alabama, she suffered for what she did. She was fired from her job within two months and her husband eventually lost his job as well. They were harassed and threatened. She went to work for the group that coordinated the boycott and began to speak for civil rights throughout the county. She and her husband eventually moved to Detroit, where she became involved in community work and continued to work for civil rights. She has been honored many times, and millions saw her appearance at the 1988 Democratic National Convention. She was hailed by Martin Luther King Jr. just before his assassination as "the great fuse that led to the modern stride toward freedom." (p. 146)

Here are the questions for students to consider:

A. What is a boycott and what effect did the bus boycott have on Alabama's business community?

B. How do you think that an individual who was relatively uninvolved in the civil rights movement could become such an important figure in that movement?

22. This excerpt comes from another high school U.S. history textbook. Alan Brinkley, *The Unfinished Nation: A Concise History of the American People* (New York: McGraw-Hill, 1997, 1993), p. 819. It is used as a model in some teacher-education programs:

On December 1, 1955, Rosa Parks, an African American woman, was arrested in Montgomery, Alabama, when she refused to give up her seat on a Montgomery bus to a white passenger (as required by the Jim Crow Laws that regulated race relations in the city and throughout most of the South). Parks, an active civil rights leader in the community, had apparently decided spontaneously to resist the order to move. The arrest of this admired woman produced outrage in the city's African-American community, which organized a boycott of the bus system to demand an end to segregated seating.

Once launched, the boycott was almost completely effective. It put economic pressure not only on the bus company (a private concern) but on many Montgomery merchants, because the bus boycotters found it difficult to get to downtown stores and tended to shop instead in their own neighborhoods. Even so, the boycott might well have failed had it not been for a Supreme Court decision late in 1956, inspired in part by the protest, that declared segregation in public transportation to be illegal. The buses in

Montgomery abandoned their discriminatory seating policies, and the boycott came to a close.

23. This excerpt is from an elementary school history textbook currently in use by James A. Banks, Barry K. Beyer, Gloria Contreras, Gloria Ladson, Mary A. McFarland, Walter C. Parker, and Jean Craven, *A New Nation: Adventures in Time and Place* (New York and Farmington: McGraw-High School Division, 2000).

In Montgomery, Alabama, in 1955 Rosa Parks said "No" when a bus driver told her to give her seat to a white person. Parks was arrested. In response, African Americans refused to ride city buses for over a year.

24. In Robert Jakoubek's *Martin Luther King Jr.,* in the series Black Americans of Achievement (New York: Chelsea House Publishers, 1989), p. 44, that is currently in many school libraries, Rosa Parks's action on the bus is described.

[O]n Tuesday evening, December 1, 1955, a small, neatly dressed black woman in Montgomery left work at quitting time, walked across the street to do some shopping at a pharmacy, and then boarded a bus for the ride home. She took a seat toward the rear, in the row just behind the section marked Whites Only. Holding her packages, she was glad to sit down. After a long day, her feet hurt.

As the bus wound its way through Montgomery, it steadily filled with passengers, and soon every seat was taken. When two white men boarded and paid their fares, the bus driver called over his shoulder for the first row of blacks to move back. After some delay, three blacks rose and stood in the aisle. But Mrs. Rosa Parks, her feet aching, her lap covered with packages, did not budge. The driver shouted, "Look woman, I told you I wanted the seat. Are you going to stand up?"

Gently but firmly, Rosa Parks said "No," and for that she was arrested and thrown in jail.

Most of the selections cited here illustrate that the "Rosa Was Tired" myth persists. Schools, and in particular school libraries, are under such fiscal pressure that they cannot buy many current books that tend to correct the historical misconceptions of Rosa Parks's role in the Civil Rights Movement. Textbooks tend to be cautious and increasingly conservative, so the militancy of people involved in the boycott is played down and the personal heroism of some people takes the place of community-based movements.

In Chapter 2, "Teaching Suggestions and Resources," some excellent books are cited and some ideas for teaching and analyzing texts written for children are included.

2

Teaching Suggestions and Resources

*T*he story of Rosa Parks and the Montgomery bus boycott has to be considered in the context of the role of racism and the legal, institutional, social, and personal constructs that existed in the South before and during the time of the boycott. It also begs retelling from different points of view. For example, what is the experience of the victims of racism— in this case African American people? What is the experience of racists—in this case many white Southerners? And what is the experience of someone who opposes racism and whose actions are shaped by the knowledge that this stance might cost them their lives? The bus boycott has to be set in a social world where challenges to white dominance, whether from the African American community alone, or from coalitions of African Americans and some whites, were a serious and dangerous matter. Teaching the story of Rosa Parks should not have a happy face. After all, she and her husband had to leave Montgomery and settle in Detroit after the boycott because they lost their jobs and were intimidated and threatened by the white racist community.

This is a delicate matter, because events like the Montgomery bus boycott can trouble young children and enrage older youth. But the world is full of trouble, and we cannot simply turn away from harsh realities or complex moral issues. We have learned this lesson from Holocaust studies—do not turn your face away from pain and madness at any age. Learn your history so you will not have to relive it.

In planning how to teach about Rosa Parks and the boycott, it is essential to think through how much time you have to devote to the subject. Every teacher faces the dilemma of too much to teach in too little time. The suggestions that follow could easily take up weeks and ideally could be articulated into a month-long civil rights curriculum, part of which would be devoted to the Montgomery bus boycott. It could also include the Selma, Alabama, march (see, for example, Charles E. Fager, *Selma, 1965* [Boston: Beacon Press, 1985]); the desegregation of schools in Little Rock, Arkansas; the lives and works of Martin Luther King Jr., Fannie Lou Hamer, and Ella Baker; the nature of the Student Non-Violent Coordinating Committee (SNCC), the NAACP, and all of the many, many other groups and individuals that played a role in eliminating legalized segregation in the South. I have deliberately stuffed as much material into this guide as I could, with the confidence that teachers can pick and choose what is useful in their own programs and will feel free to adjust, add, subtract, shape, and re-create what is provided here. This is the opposite of the move these days to provide those of us who teach with a scripted, "teacher-proof" curriculum, which disrespects and insults us, and assumes that we have neither the judgment, experience, or intelligence to build curricula for our students. This is an attempt to provide the basic material to *build* a curriculum rather than be trapped by it.

The Vocabulary of Teaching Human Rights and Civil Rights

One way to begin, in almost every teaching context where there is a sense of social justice, is with the vocabulary that is central to understanding the issues raised in the struggle for human rights. Teaching vocabulary is not simply about learning new words so students will do well on standardized tests. At its best, it is a way of introducing young people to concepts and ideas they may vaguely know but have not articulated or encountered in the language-impoverished world of TV, video games, and hurried family lives, where time for discussion is minimized because of adult fatigue or absence.

Here is one take on an annotated, basic teaching vocabulary involving clusters of words that could set the context for helping students develop a more complex understanding of the Montgomery bus boycott, the Civil Rights Movement, and other struggles for human rights, past and present. Of course, this is just one short list and it is very important for teachers to create their own lists as well, to modify anything they are given to teach, and to shape their curriculum in the service of their particular students.

A *Teaching Vocabulary for Rosa Parks and the Montgomery Bus Boycott*

Narrative Stance—This concept has to do with who tells the story. It is not just a matter of fictional narrative, but, in this case, of historical narrative. There are a number of ways to introduce this concept to students. For example, recently I was asked to introduce a unit on *Huckleberry Finn* to an urban high school class. There are many sensitive issues in the book, particularly when it comes to issues of race. The narrator of the book is Huck himself, and we see the story unfold from his point of view, which is basically an abolitionist perspective. I came up with the idea of supplementing Huck's stance with Jim's and asked students to rewrite part of the tale with Jim as the narrator. Looking at the story from Jim's perspective is a way of showing him as a thinking, troubled person in flight from oppression. The students, not surprisingly, came up with some powerful insights into issues of racism, resistance, and defiance.

The story of Rosa Parks has been told by many people, and in studying the works it is important to call students' attention not just to the story, but to who is telling it, what they choose to include, and what they leave out.

Human Rights—The question of human rights is central to Rosa Parks's story. This issue comes up over and over with respect to Mrs. Parks's fight for respect, dignity, and the rights of all people to the privileges of the dominant white community in the Montgomery of her time.

The first workshop Rosa Parks attended at Highlander was

centered on the implementation of the *Brown* decision declaring the illegality of segregated schools. Eleanor Roosevelt also attended that workshop. In 1948, Mrs. Roosevelt, widow of President Franklin D. Roosevelt, was chairperson of an eight-person committee that drafted the United Nations Universal Declaration of Human Rights.

The final document was one of the texts used at the Highlander workshop that Mrs. Parks and Mrs. Roosevelt attended, and the very notion of universal human rights affirmed by the United Nations played a role in the development of the Civil Rights Movement, which in many ways was part of the worldwide anti-colonial movement of the 1950s and 1960s.

Following is a copy of the Universal Declaration of Human Rights, which might be useful as discussions develop about the context, not only about the Montgomery bus boycott, but of the entire Civil Rights Movement. Articles 1 and 2 are particularly important, as they validate on an international scale everyone's "rights to the fruits of the tree of life."

Universal Declaration of Human Rights
Adopted and proclaimed by General Assembly resolution 217 A (III) of 10 December 1948

On December 10, 1948, the General Assembly of the United Nations adopted and proclaimed the Universal Declaration of Human Rights. . . . Following this historic act the Assembly called upon all Member countries to publicize the text of the Declaration and "to cause it to be disseminated, displayed, read and expounded principally in schools and other educational institutions, without distinction based on the political status of countries or territories."

PREAMBLE

Whereas recognition of the inherent dignity and of the equal and inalienable rights of all members of the human family is the foundation of freedom, justice and peace in the world,

Whereas disregard and contempt for human rights have resulted in barbarous acts which have outraged the conscience of mankind, and the advent of a world in which human beings shall enjoy freedom of speech and belief and freedom from fear and want has been proclaimed as the highest aspiration of the common people,

Whereas it is essential, if man is not to be compelled to have recourse, as a last resort, to rebellion against tyranny and oppression, that human rights should be protected by the rule of law,

Whereas it is essential to promote the development of friendly relations between nations,

Whereas the peoples of the United Nations have in the Charter reaffirmed their faith in fundamental human rights, in the dignity and worth of the human person and in the equal rights of men and women and have determined to promote social progress and better standards of life in larger freedom,

Whereas Member States have pledged themselves to

achieve, in co-operation with the United Nations, the promotion of universal respect for and observance of human rights and fundamental freedoms,

Whereas a common understanding of these rights and freedoms is of the greatest importance for the full realization of this pledge,

Now, Therefore THE GENERAL ASSEMBLY proclaims THIS UNIVERSAL DECLARATION OF HUMAN RIGHTS as a common standard of achievement for all peoples and all nations, to the end that every individual and every organ of society, keeping this Declaration constantly in mind, shall strive by teaching and education to promote respect for these rights and freedoms and by progressive measures, national and international, to secure their universal and effective recognition and observance, both among the peoples of Member States themselves and among the peoples of territories under their jurisdiction.

Article 1.

All human beings are born free and equal in dignity and rights. They are endowed with reason and conscience and should act towards one another in a spirit of brotherhood.

Article 2.

Everyone is entitled to all the rights and freedoms set forth in this Declaration, without distinction of any kind, such as race, colour, sex, language, religion, political or other opinion, national or social origin, property, birth or other status. Furthermore, no distinction shall be made on the basis of the political, jurisdictional or international status of the country or territory to which a person belongs, whether it be independent, trust, non-self-governing or under any other limitation of sovereignty.

Article 3.

Everyone has the right to life, liberty and security of person.

Article 4.

No one shall be held in slavery or servitude; slavery and the slave trade shall be prohibited in all their forms.

Article 5.

No one shall be subjected to torture or to cruel, inhuman or degrading treatment or punishment.

Article 6.

Everyone has the right to recognition everywhere as a person before the law.

Article 7.

All are equal before the law and are entitled without any discrimination to equal protection of the law. All are entitled to equal protection against any discrimination in violation of this Declaration and against any incitement to such discrimination.

Article 8.

Everyone has the right to an effective remedy by the competent national tribunals for acts violating the fundamental rights granted him by the constitution or by law.

Article 9.

No one shall be subjected to arbitrary arrest, detention or exile.

Article 10.

Everyone is entitled in full equality to a fair and public hearing by an independent and impartial tribunal, in the determination of his rights and obligations and of any criminal charge against him.

Article 11.

1. Everyone charged with a penal offence has the right to be presumed innocent until proved guilty according to law in a public trial at which he has had all the guarantees necessary for his defence.
2. No one shall be held guilty of any penal offence on account of any act or omission which did not constitute a penal offence, under national or international law, at the time when it was committed. Nor shall a heavier penalty be imposed than the one that was applicable at the time the penal offence was committed.

Article 12.

No one shall be subjected to arbitrary interference with his privacy, family, home or correspondence, nor to attacks upon his honour and reputation. Everyone has the right to the protection of the law against such interference or attacks.

Article 13.

1. Everyone has the right to freedom of movement and residence within the borders of each state.
2. Everyone has the right to leave any country, including his own, and to return to his country.

Article 14.

1. Everyone has the right to seek and to enjoy in other countries asylum from persecution.
2. This right may not be invoked in the case of prosecutions genuinely arising from non-political crimes or from acts contrary to the purposes and principles of the United Nations.

Article 15.

1. Everyone has the right to a nationality.
2. No one shall be arbitrarily deprived of his nationality nor denied the right to change his nationality.

Article 16.

1. Men and women of full age, without any limitation due to race, nationality or religion, have the right to marry and to found a family. They are entitled to equal rights as to marriage, during marriage and at its dissolution.
2. Marriage shall be entered into only with the free and full consent of the intending spouses.
3. The family is the natural and fundamental group unit of society and is entitled to protection by society and the State.

Article 17.

1. Everyone has the right to own property alone as well as in association with others.
2. No one shall be arbitrarily deprived of his property.

Article 18.

Everyone has the right to freedom of thought, conscience and religion; this right includes freedom to change his religion or belief, and freedom, either alone or in community with others and in public or private, to manifest his religion or belief in teaching, practice, worship and observance.

Article 19.

Everyone has the right to freedom of opinion and expression; this right includes freedom to hold opinions without interference and to seek, receive and impart information and ideas through any media and regardless of frontiers.

Article 20.

1. Everyone has the right to freedom of peaceful assembly and association.
2. No one may be compelled to belong to an association.

Article 21.

1. Everyone has the right to take part in the government of his country, directly or through freely chosen representatives.
2. Everyone has the right of equal access to public service in his country.
3. The will of the people shall be the basis of the authority of government; this will shall be expressed in periodic and genuine elections which shall be by universal and equal suffrage and shall be held by secret vote or by equivalent free voting procedures.

Article 22.

Everyone, as a member of society, has the right to social security and is entitled to realization, through national effort and international co-operation and in accordance with the organization and resources of each State, of the economic, social and cultural rights indispensable for his dignity and the free development of his personality.

Article 23.

1. Everyone has the right to work, to free choice of employment, to just and favourable conditions of work and to protection against unemployment.
2. Everyone, without any discrimination, has the right to equal pay for equal work.
3. Everyone who works has the right to just and favourable remuneration ensuring for himself and his family an existence worthy of human dignity, and supplemented, if necessary, by other means of social protection.
4. Everyone has the right to form and to join trade unions for the protection of his interests.

Article 24.

Everyone has the right to rest and leisure, including reasonable limitation of working hours and periodic holidays with pay.

Article 25.

1. Everyone has the right to a standard of living adequate for the health and well-being of himself and of his family, including food, clothing, housing and medical care and necessary social services, and the right to security in the event of unemployment, sickness, disability, widowhood, old age or other lack of livelihood in circumstances beyond his control.
2. Motherhood and childhood are entitled to special care

and assistance. All children, whether born in or out of wedlock, shall enjoy the same social protection.

Article 26.

1. Everyone has the right to education. Education shall be free, at least in the elementary and fundamental stages. Elementary education shall be compulsory. Technical and professional education shall be made generally available and higher education shall be equally accessible to all on the basis of merit.

2. Education shall be directed to the full development of the human personality and to the strengthening of respect for human rights and fundamental freedoms. It shall promote understanding, tolerance and friendship among all nations, racial or religious groups, and shall further the activities of the United Nations for the maintenance of peace.

3. Parents have a prior right to choose the kind of education that shall be given to their children.

Article 27.

1. Everyone has the right freely to participate in the cultural life of the community, to enjoy the arts and to share in scientific advancement and its benefits.

2. Everyone has the right to the protection of the moral and material interests resulting from any scientific, literary or artistic production of which he is the author.

Article 28.

Everyone is entitled to a social and international order in which the rights and freedoms set forth in this Declaration can be fully realized.

Article 29.

1. Everyone has duties to the community in which alone the free and full development of his personality is possible.
2. In the exercise of his rights and freedoms, everyone shall be subject only to such limitations as are determined by law solely for the purpose of securing due recognition and respect for the rights and freedoms of others and of meeting the just requirements of morality, public order and the general welfare in a democratic society.
3. These rights and freedoms may in no case be exercised contrary to the purposes and principles of the United Nations.

Article 30.

Nothing in this Declaration may be interpreted as implying for any State, group or person any right to engage in any activity or to perform any act aimed at the destruction of any of the rights and freedoms set forth herein.

Racism, Segregation—Segregation is best understood in the context of the larger issue of racism. The segregation of the buses in Montgomery was just one manifestation of racism in that city. Libraries were segregated, as were restaurants, hotels, swimming pools, water fountains, movie theaters, and all other public and private facilities. The daily humiliation as well as the physical threats experienced by African Americans, beginning with slavery, were palpable, everyday experiences. In this context, the acts of Rosa Parks and all the other people involved in the boycott can be understood as moral actions in the face of great peril. Two books are especially useful in guiding teachers as they deal with sensitive issues such as racism. The first is by Louise Dehrman-Sparks and Carol Brunson Phillip, *Teaching/Learning Anti-racism* (New York: Teachers College Press, Columbia University, 1997). Although this book refers to teaching anti-racist education in college, I have used it in elementary, middle, and high school as well by adjusting the lessons in the book to make them age appropriate. *Teaching/Learning Anti-racism* presents both a compassionate and thorough way of exploring racism and then overcoming it. My students in teacher-education courses have found it useful not only to themselves but also, after translations into age appropriate uses, to their students.

The second valuable book is by John Langone, *Spreading Poison: A Book about Racism and Prejudice* (Boston: Little, Brown, 1993), which, in addition to discussing racism directed against African Americans, considers anti-Semitism, homophobia, sexism, and anti-immigrant sentiments. The book is written for high school students as well as adult readers and is full of examples and suggestions about how to undo racism.

In terms of the specific focus on the Montgomery bus boycott, there are some facts that when inserted into classroom lessons, would set the boycott in the larger context of racism. Montgomery, Alabama, was the capital of the Confederacy, and some people in the community believe it still is. Number 1 Dexter Avenue is the address of the state capitol building. It was the site, in 1861, of the inauguration of Jefferson Davis as president of the Confederacy. Dexter Avenue King Memorial Baptist Church, at 454 Dexter Avenue, is the place where E.D. Nixon called the meeting in 1955 that launched the bus boycott. About twenty years ago, I had a chance to visit the Dexter Avenue Church and was overwhelmed to discover that from its steps I could see the capitol building and the Confederate flag that was still flying from its dome. This has made me wonder whether Nixon announced the boycott partially because of King's ministry at the church and partially to make a public statement that racism was not to be tolerated any longer in Montgomery. Segregation was legal in Montgomery at the time, and Nixon, Rosa Parks, Jo Anne Gibson Robinson, and others involved in the boycott were asserting that moral laws overrode statute when the issue was social justice.

Boycott / Non-violent Protest—To study the Montgomery bus boycott, students must know what a boycott is. The word "boycott" is derived from an actual person. Captain Boycott from Mayo, Ireland, was a land agent, that is, a landlord, who, during the 1880s, refused to reduce rents to poor tenants who were the ones most likely to be overcharged. As a way of getting even with Boycott, the people of Mayo ostracized him. Most likely it became impossible for him even to buy a pint of beer in the local pub; people refused to do business with him, which is similar to what the African American community in Montgomery did with the bus company. The people of Mayo boycotted Captain Boycott and the black community boycotted the bus company.

It is very important to explain to students the meaning of a boycott, since the *response* to a non-violent boycott can often be violent, as happened in the Montgomery bus boycott and the grape boycott led by Cesar Chavez in the 1970s. It makes sense to illustrate the power of non-violent protest despite the violence that protesters might face for their peaceful actions. Other instances of organized non-violence—as cited in the previous examples, in Martin Luther King Jr.'s life, in the role Mahatma Gandhi played in the struggle for India's independence, and in Nelson Mandela's struggle for South Africa's liberation— provide instances that illuminate the events in Montgomery and place Rosa Parks's action in an international context. This could contribute to students' understanding of their own lives as citizens of a democracy.

Leadership / Heroism / Participation—When assessing a movement, it is important to look at the varied roles people play in effecting change. Leadership, in the case of the Montgomery bus boycott, resides in people like E.D. Nixon and Joanne Robinson; heroism and sacrifice are left to the few charismatic figures like Rosa Parks and Martin Luther King Jr., and participation is available to everyone. None of the three stand alone, and the study of social action must show appropriate respect for and understanding of the courage of all participants in a movement. These three concepts can and should be taught together rather than teaching just the stories of individual heroism. The participants are too easily left out; without them there would be no movement.

Information: Phone Trees / Pamphlets / Other Media—Finally, the role of information is crucial in the development of a movement. Without the use of phone trees in Montgomery, or the 50,000 pamphlets that Joanne Robinson produced, or all of the information passed on in barber shops, beauty parlors, and other informal gathering places where African Americans could communicate without white surveillance, there could not have been a boycott.

In addition to holding discussions, students can engage in community-based projects designed to develop participation in social action movements. They can write pamphlets, develop phone trees, and, these days, develop Web sites, chat rooms, and blogs to create a constituency for positive changes they would like to make happen in their communities.

Comparing Texts

Teaching about Rosa Parks and the bus boycott often requires undoing students' stereotypes and helping them reconstruct their knowledge and ideas based on new information. One way to do this is to compare different texts that treat the same events. In the case of Rosa Parks and the Montgomery bus boycott, we can examine all of the textbooks used in schools and children's books in the school library or in the local public library. Placing the texts side by side, students will be able to notice the contrast between Rosa Parks the "tired," and Rosa Parks the "activist." Listed below are a number of fairly recent books about Rosa Parks that show Mrs. Parks in a more rounded way than almost all of the texts I mentioned in the Appendix in Chapter 1.

Suggested Reading

Adler, David A. *A Picture Book of Rosa Parks*. New York: Holiday House, 1993.

Greenfield, Eloise. *Rosa Parks*. New York: HarperCollins, 1995.

Raymond, Della. *Martin Luther King, Jr.: The Dream of Peaceful Revolution*. New York: Silver Burdett Press, 1990.

Ringgold, Faith. *If a Bus Could Talk: The Story of Rosa Parks*. New York: Simon and Schuster, 1999.

Smith, Jessie Carney, ed. *Black Heroes of the 20th Century*. New York: Visible Ink, 1998.

Curriculum

Another way to approach the story is by developing a curriculum that sets the boycott in the social, cultural, and economic conditions of Montgomery at the time of the boycott. This can be done in a complex way with a consideration of the Jim Crow laws and voter registration drives, sentiments characteristic of the white power structure in the city, and the importance of buses to transportation there. Three specific things can be done here: (1) study Montgomery as "the capital of the Confederacy"; (2) research and discuss the nature and history of Jim Crow and Jim Crow laws; and (3) obtain maps of Montgomery. (Use a bus route map from the 1950s to enable students to identify sites such as the state capitol, Martin Luther King Jr.'s church, the department store where Rosa Parks worked, the bus stop where she got on the bus, the union office of E.D. Nixon, the college where Joanne Robinson taught, and so forth.) By studying maps and tracing routes, political contrasts will be manifested in the landscape, thus bringing the story to life.

Utilize the Internet to research and download information about neglected issues. Research projects can then be developed by organizing groups of students to explore one of the issues and then present their findings to their fellow students. Here's a case where the Internet definitely has substantial educational value.

International Comparisons

It is also possible to approach the bus boycott by studying the anatomy of racism on a worldwide level. This means looking at the history and overthrow of apartheid in South Africa, the Holocaust, the Armenian genocide, and other events in recent history. It is essential for students to understand that people exist who will slaughter other ethnic and racial groups in order to maintain what they consider their own racial superiority. At the same time, it is crucial to show that there are resisters, people of all races who continue to fight for social justice and risk their lives—as did Rosa Parks—to maintain their values and advocate justice. In this context, Rosa Parks can be understood as someone who in effect risked her life for her values. And students should know that Mrs. Parks did not live happily ever after in Montgomery but was forced to move to Detroit because of death threats against her life and that of her family.

Non-violent Protest

An alternative way to set the context for teaching about Rosa Parks and the bus boycott is to begin with a study of civil disobedience and non-violent protest. Writers such as Henry David Thoreau and Gandhi, as well as some of the speeches and writings of Martin Luther King Jr., and the actions of Cesar Chavez, can introduce the Civil Rights Movement and the actions of Rosa Parks. She performed no act of violence and never tried to. She acted on the basis of conscience and simply refused to obey laws she considered unjust. The concepts of conscience and non-violence are rarely taught specifically in school, though here is a perfect opportunity to place the boycott beside other instances of resistance to injustice that do not resort to duplicating the violence of the unjust.

One of my favorite ways to introduce the concept of conscience for high school students is to begin with this poem by the Irish poet Seamus Heaney. It requires close reading and discussion but, as I have discovered when reading it with students, it dramatically and effectively points up what having a conscience is all about:

Seamus Heaney, "The Republic of Conscience"

I

When I landed in the republic of conscience
it was so noiseless when the engines stopped
I could hear a curlew high above the runway.

At immigration, the clerk was an old man
who produced a wallet from his homespun coat
and showed me a photograph of his grandfather.

The woman in customs asked me to declare
the words of our traditional cures and charms
to cure dumbness and heal the evil eye.

No porters. No interpreters. No taxi.
You carried your own burden and very soon
your symptoms of creeping privilege disappeared.

II

Fog is a dreaded omen there but lightning
spells universal good and parents hang
swaddled infants in trees during thunderstorms.

Salt is their precious mineral. And seashells
are held to the ear during births and funerals,
The base of all inks and pigments is seawater.

The sacred symbol is a stylized boat.
The sail is an ear, the mast a sloping pen,
The hull a mouth-shape, the keel an open eye.

At their inauguration, public leaders
must swear to uphold unwritten law and weep
to atone for their presumption to hold office—

and to affirm their faith that all life sprang
from salt in tears which the sky-god wept
after he dreamt his solitude was endless.

III

I came back from that frugal republic
with my two arms the one length, the customs woman
having insisted my allowance was myself.

The old man rose and gazed into my face
and said that was official recognition
that I was now a dual citizen.

He therefore desired me when I got home
to consider myself a representative
and to speak on their behalf in my own tongue.

Their embassies, he said, were everywhere
but operated independently
and no ambassador would ever be relieved.

Multimedia

In the course of studying the bus boycott, students can produce
a play, DVD, or video that focuses on several specific events
that took place during the boycott. Events can be:

Mrs. Parks refusing to move.

Mrs. Parks discussing the boycott with E.D. Nixon.

Mrs. Parks being fingerprinted and booked into jail, then being bailed out.

Joanne Robinson and her colleagues and students setting up the phone trees and printing and distributing 50,000 pamphlets.

Conversations between E.D. Nixon and Martin Luther King Jr. about the community choosing to use his church for a meeting.

Rosa Parks leaving Montgomery for Detroit.

The Highlander Center workshop Rosa Parks attended (for information about this, consult Myles Horton, *The Long Haul* [New York: Teachers College, Columbia Press, 1990]).

The idea here is to avoid focusing exclusively on Rosa Parks, while at the same time acknowledging her courage and central role in the events in Montgomery.

Visual Arts

Create a mural depicting the events during the bus boycott. This would involve students doing book and Internet research to find out what all of the people involved looked like. Be sure that the white community is not neglected in the unfolding of the events: this would include the Ku Klux Klan, quiet citizens, the political establishment that had to deal with the boycott, the police, and the few white allies of the African American community.

One way to do this might be to create a scroll that enfolds the story frame by frame. Another would be to find a way to include all of the events in one large painting. If you cannot paint directly on the wall, quarter-inch plywood panels will do. The mural can be temporarily displayed and then taken down. One advantage of this method is that new groups of students can develop their own visual depictions of the events in Montgomery. If you choose to do this, be sure to document each mural and develop a Rosa Parks mural scrapbook so graduates can see their own work and new students can see what has already been done in order to imagine new ways to make their own statements.

Community Activism

As a follow-up to the study of the boycott, students can find community issues involving social justice that they might want to work on. Some issues might be supporting a food bank, making representations to the school board about school problems that students would like to see solved, working with community groups about questions of police or gang violence, helping health care workers, or developing a lobby for student rights. Of course, these issues will differ from community to community, but it is important for students to apply their learning to collective action and to act for social justice if they believe in it. It also doesn't hurt to learn how to develop a telephone tree, create a Listserv, and learn how to print and distribute pamphlets.

Mobilizing for social justice would certainly be in the spirit of the Montgomery bus boycott.

Rosa Parks after the Boycott

Finally, it is possible to study what Rosa Parks faced when she moved to Detroit. It makes sense to examine this in the context of the great northern migrations during the 1940s and 1950s, when tens of thousands of African Americans moved out of the South. A resource for this is the painter Jacob Lawrence's migration series, which tells, in visual form, the story of the journey northward and the situations African Americans faced when they arrived in the North. Jim Crow, economic opportunity, and a journey toward hope all had a role in the move north.

In addition, later in her life Rosa Parks worked in the Detroit office of Representative John Conyers for years. In this context, it would make sense to research John Conyers and find out what ideas he represents (it is possible to find some of his speeches and interviews on the Internet). It is also worth exploring what role Rosa Parks played when she worked for Conyers. One place to start would be to read Mrs. Parks's autobiography. Another would be to examine the role of local offices for members of the House of Representatives. Students could visit the offices, meet the staff, and find out how elected officials keep in touch with the people who elected them as well as how they function in Washington, D.C. This is another way to help students become involved in the process of making and understanding democracy.

3

Close Bonds: The Strength of Three Women

Cynthia Brown

I asked Cynthia Brown, an old friend and colleague, to write a short article that would give readers a closer look at Rosa Parks and the women who influenced her. Dr. Brown, who is a professor at Dominican College in San Raphael, California, is the author and editor of a number of books including Ready from Within: Septima Clark and the Civil Rights Movement, *an oral biography and* Like It Was: A Complete Guide to Writing Oral History. *She is also a former Highlander director and teacher of Rosa Parks. Cynthia was a close friend of Septima Clark and Virginia Durr and was kind enough to share her understanding of their work and of the relationship they had with Rosa Parks in the following article.*

In May 1980, Rosa Parks came to Oakland, California, to be honored at a dinner to raise funds for the Highlander Research and Education Center in Tennessee. It was the twenty-fifth anniversary of the Montgomery bus boycott, and people in the Bay Area were eager to see the legendary Mrs. Parks.

I was among those who helped escort Mrs. Parks to the dinner. In the restroom she straightened herself up before the ordeal of meeting with reporters and photographers. To our amazement, when she pulled out the hairpins that held the braids around her head, her hair fell in thick cascades of waves to her waist.

Seeing our astonished faces, Mrs. Parks explained that since her husband Raymond liked her hair long, she had never been able to cut it, even though it was a lot of trouble. Besides, her ancestors included Native Americans, whom she honored with her braids.

Rosa McCauley Parks's father, James McCauley, was the grandson of a part Native American, part African slave girl, and a Yankee soldier. Parks's mother, Leona Edwards, was born to parents who were both partly white. Edwards' father, Sylvester Edwards, could have passed for white. He was born to a white slave owner and a mixed slave housekeeper. They both died when he was young, and Sylvester had been so mistreated by the overseer who took over that Sylvester grew up with an intense hatred for white people. He instilled in his daughters and grandchildren that you don't put up with bad treatment from anybody; he did not have the meek attitude that Parks found common among African Americans (*My Life*, pp. 14–15, 59).

Yet, as Parks grew up on her maternal grandparents' eighteen-acre farm in Pine Level, forty miles south of Montgomery, she came to realize that not all white people were hateful. "When I was very young, I remember, there was an old, old white lady who used to take me fishing. She was real nice and treated us just like anybody else. She used to visit my grand-parents a lot, and talk with them for a long time, so there were some good white people in Pine Level" (*My Life*, p. 37).

By the time the bus boycott got underway in December 1955, Mrs. Parks had a group of supporters almost as diverse as her ancestors. She had her congregation at St. Paul's AME church, and her close black friends, E.D. Nixon and Johnnie Mae Carr, along with Fred Gray, a twenty-four-year-old attor-ney fresh out of Case Western Reserve Law School, and Martin Luther King Jr., the twenty-six-year-old minister who had been at Dexter Avenue Baptist Church for fourteen months. Parks had a close white friend, Virginia Durr, and a white neighbor, Robert Graetz, the twenty-seven-year-old pastor of a black Lutheran church across the street from her. Three months earlier she had found two new mentors at Highlander Center in Tennessee and had made friends with them: Myles Horton and Septima Clark.

Of these relationships, Parks's friendship with Carr and Nixon went back the furthest—with Carr to their school days when they were ages eight to twelve, and with Nixon back to the early 1940s, when she began working with him in the NAACP. Her friendship with Durr only went back about a year and a half to when Nixon introduced them to each other. From then on the two women had managed to conduct a true friend-ship in Jim Crow Montgomery, an amazing act of courage and ingenuity.

Virginia, with her husband Clifford, had returned to Mont-gomery in spring 1951, when Virginia was forty-eight years old. Montgomery was Clifford's hometown, while Virginia had grown up in Birmingham. For seventeen years they had lived in a suburb of Washington, D.C., where Clifford had worked as a lawyer for the New Deal. Clifford left Washington on principle; he refused to enforce the loyalty oath among his agency's employees. When the Durrs returned to Montgomery after an interim year in Denver, they had exhausted their savings and had to move in with Clifford's mother, Lucy Judkins Durr.

Virginia Durr had grown up with her family's traditional white, aristocratic, racist attitudes, but, during her years in Washington she changed her mind about Southern segregation. She came to believe that it should end immediately; she also believed all adult women and African Americans should be able to vote, which they were prevented from doing in the South by the poll tax. To achieve her goals, Durr worked in the women's division of the Democratic Party, the Southern Conference for Human Welfare, and chaired the National Committee to End the Poll Tax.

Living with her mother-in-law, a perfect example of the traditional Southern white lady, Durr felt constrained to limit her activities and the expression of her opinions. "I hadn't said anything controversial to anybody for two or three years, quite a long time for me to stay silent," she said in her autobiography (*Outside the Magic Circle*, p. 244).

Clifford set up a law practice, with Virginia as his secretary. He represented the Durr Drug Company, headed by his brother, and took cases referred by E.D. Nixon, president of the local NAACP, of black people beaten up in jail or charged 500 percent interest on loans. The people bringing these cases had no money; those who had money went to more powerful white attorneys. The Durrs barely managed to survive financially during their first years back in Montgomery.

The Durrs liked E.D. Nixon a lot. Virginia thought he was "an honest, forthright kind of fellow. I got to know his wife very well, too—the sweetest, prettiest thing you ever saw, just a lovely woman" (*Outside the Magic Circle*, p. 252).

Like many of the few Southerners who overtly supported the end of segregation, Virginia Durr was accused of being a Communist. Politicians used the public's fear of Communism to help win elections. The National Committee to Abolish the Poll Tax, which Durr had led from 1941 to 1948, had accepted donations from some groups and individuals who may have been Communists, and this was enough to level accusations at her.

Jim Eastland, a senator from Mississippi, chaired a Senate committee charged with investigating possible Communists. In spring 1954, wanting to discredit the Supreme Court before it issued its decision on school desegregation, he subpoenaed Durr, among others, and held a hearing in New Orleans. He hired an ex-Communist to testify that Mrs. Durr had full knowledge, through her friendship with Eleanor Roosevelt, of a Communist spy ring operating inside the White House. The lies and unfair procedures of the hearing were so apparent that news reporters sided with the defendants, and Eastland called off his plans for a second hearing (*Refusing Racism*, p. 41). To avoid possible cross burnings at Clifford Durr's parental home, the Durrs moved into their own apartment, giving Virginia the independence to pursue her own interests.

In April, when the Supreme Court handed down its decision

in *Brown v. Board of Education of Topeka, Kansas,* against segregation in public schools, the Durrs had three daughters in public schools in Montgomery. Lucy was seventeen, Tillah was twelve or thirteen, and Lulah was six. Virginia's sister, Josephine Foster Black, had married Hugo Black, a lawyer from Birmingham who had been on the Supreme Court since 1937, so the Durrs' daughters were nieces of a justice who was causing this calamity, as most white people in Montgomery saw it. One of Tillah's teachers told her, in front of the whole class: "You just tell your uncle that I'm not going to teach any nigger children. I don't care how many laws they pass" (*Outside the Magic Circle*, p. 269).

Sometime early in the post-*Brown* period, E.D. Nixon felt he had gotten to know Virginia Durr well enough to introduce her to Rosa Parks. Once, when Durr was at his house, Nixon drove over to pick up Parks and brought her back to his house to meet Durr (*My Life*, p. 95).

At the time, Mrs. Parks was living in a cubbyhole apartment at the Cleveland Courts housing project two miles away from Durr, with her mother and her husband, Raymond Parks, a barber at the Atlas Barber Shop, who shaved and cut the hair of high-class whites. Mrs. Parks worked full time as a seamstress at the Montgomery Fair department store where, for $25 a week, she altered the clothes that white people bought. (Black people could buy clothes at the store, but they could not try them on or have them altered.)

When Durr learned that Parks was an expert seamstress, she hired her to do some sewing in the evenings after work. Durr later remembered that she would take boxes of hand-me-down clothes that she received from her sister, Josephine Black, to Mrs. Parks to alter for her daughters. They would sit and talk for hours. Parks remembered doing the alterations and sewing a trousseau for Lucy Durr before her wedding in the summer of 1957. The women became intimate friends, despite having to call each other Mrs. Parks and Mrs. Durr. Durr, of course, couldn't call Parks "Rosa" until Parks could call her "Virginia," and that took another twenty years (*My Life*, pp. 95–6; *Outside the Magic Circle*, p. 253).

"She [Rosa Parks] is very quiet, determined, brave and frugal, not [at] all sophisticated and very churchgoing and orthodox in most of her thinking," Durr wrote her old friend, Jessica Mitford, about her new friend. "But thoroughly good and brave, and the people here have the highest respect for her. When she feels at ease and gets relaxed, she can show a delightful sense of humor, but it is not often" (*Mine Eyes*, p. 86).

Durr invited Parks to join an integrated prayer group of churchwomen, who met to pray, sing, and drink a cup of tea together. These United Church Women included Mrs. Coretta Scott King and Mrs. Juanita Abernathy. Parks remembered that they sometimes met at Durr's house; Durr remembered meeting in black churches, perhaps later on when they grew to be about a hundred women from all over the state.

Women trying to be friends by praying and drinking tea proved too threatening to the white men of Montgomery. A retired admiral, John Crommelin, published a right-wing, anti-Semitic paper called *Sheet Lightening,* and in one edition he published the names, addresses, and phone numbers of everyone at the prayer meeting, which he got by taking down the license plate numbers from their parked cars. The women received harassing calls at night, and their husbands got calls from people threatening to stop doing business with them. Several husbands, brothers, and fathers took out notices in the newspaper disassociating themselves from their own women. The group never met again (*My Life*, p. 96; *Outside the Magic Circle*, p. 245).

The Durrs maintained a friendship with Myles Horton, the founder of the Highlander Center in the mountains of Tennessee just north of Alabama. The Durrs visited there several times in the forties. Virginia "developed into one of our favorite visiting teachers," wrote Horton, who liked to go fishing with Clifford. Virginia wished she had a million dollars to endow Highlander, for it was the only place in the South where people of any race could eat together and spend the night (*Refusing Racism*, pp. 42–3).

After the *Brown* decision, leaders at Highlander planned summer workshops to develop leaders for dismantling segregation. For the summer of 1955, they planned one called "Radical Desegregation: Implementing the Supreme Court Decision."

Down in Montgomery, black leaders focused on the segregated seating on buses, their number one grievance. In March 1955 police arrested Claudette Colvin, a fifteen-year-old girl, for refusing to give up her seat on the bus. Parks knew Colvin's relatives and persuaded her to join the NAACP Youth Council. The possible lawsuit against segregation on buses consumed black leaders' attention during the spring and early summer. In July, the United States Court of Appeals for the Fourth Circuit ruled that segregated bus seating was unconstitutional. Parks and other black leaders in Montgomery realized that if they could find the right plaintiff, they could desegregate Montgomery's buses (*Mine Eyes*, pp. 88–90).

Horton called Durr from Highlander to seek her advice about who in Montgomery might be the right person for a scholarship to the two-week workshop on desegregation. Without hesitation, Durr recommended Parks and drove right over to explain to her how wonderful it was at Highlander and how it was training a new generation of civil rights activists.

Eager to go, Parks confessed she could not afford the $15 for a roundtrip bus ticket to Chattanooga. Since Durr couldn't afford it either, she secured the money from a friend, Aubrey Williams. Parks arranged for a two-week leave from the Montgomery Fair department store and for her husband to cook for her mother in her absence (*Mine Eyes*, pp. 93–4; *My Life*, p. 102).

For two weeks in July and August 1954, Parks joined forty-seven other participants in formal and informal discussions during meals and recreation time. Everyone slept in bunk beds in men's and women's dormitories and ate meals together cooked by the white staff, surrounded by the cool mountain air and vistas.

Afterwards, Parks loved to tell the story of how Myles Horton explained the inexplicable phenomenon of how he got black and white people to eat together, considered impossible by most Southern people. "These reporters were asking him, 'How do you get the two races to eat together?' And he says, 'First, the food is prepared. Second, it's put on the table. Third, we ring the bell.' I find myself just cracking up many times." Parks felt that Horton had "melted a lot of my hostility and prejudice and feeling of bitterness against the white Southerner because he had such a wonderful sense of humor. . . . I found myself laughing when I hadn't been able to laugh in a long time" (speech in Berkeley, May 1, 1980).

Parks loved the experience of whites catering to her after so many years of catering to them. "One of my greatest pleasures there was enjoying the smell of bacon frying and coffee brewing and knowing that white folks were doing the preparing instead of me" (*My Life*, p. 105).

At the workshop, Parks heard Dr. Fred Patterson give a fascinating seminar. As president of Tuskegee Institute, he was a scholar she had long admired. But beyond the intellectual stimulation, "It was quite enjoyable to be with the people at Highlander. We forgot about what color anybody was. I was forty two years old, and it was one of the few times in my life up to that point when I did not feel any hostility from white people. I experienced people of different races and backgrounds meeting together in workshops and living together in peace and harmony. I felt that [I] could explain myself honestly, without any repercussions or antagonistic attitudes from other people." (*My Life*, p. 105–7)

All the staff at Highlander was white except for Septima Poinsette Clark, who ran the workshops. For Parks, getting to know Mrs. Clark, who was fifteen years her elder, became a deeply significant part of the Highlander experience.

Clark lived in Charleston, South Carolina, where she taught reading in elementary school. She had hoped to attend college, but her parents were not able to pay for it. She helped fight for equal pay for black teachers through the NAACP, and she was a friend of Judge Waties Waring, who ruled in 1948 that primary elections have to be open to all voters. Clark had been to High-lander for the first time in April 1954 and then two more times in the summer of 1954. She was helping Horton and Esau Jenkins create "citizenship schools" on Johns Island, off the coast of Charleston, where black adults could learn to read enough to register to vote. A year later she would be fired from her teaching job in Charleston for refusing to give up her membership in the NAACP, and Horton would hire her to come to Highlander. The first citizenship school opened in January 1957, and Clark then coordinated their expansion throughout the South.

At the workshop in late summer 1957, Clark found Parks shy at first. She wouldn't talk in the large group meetings, but in the dorm at night she began to tell about her experiences in Montgomery: the obscene phone calls because she was president of her youth group; the cruel incidents on the buses; the triumph of having her youth group go through the Freedom Train, sent from Washington, D.C., with an original U.S. Constitution and Declaration of Independence, requiring integrated attendance. As Clark told it, the next day, she said, "Rosa, tell these people how you got that Freedom Train to come to Montgomery. She hated to tell it. She thought that certainly someone would go back and tell the white people. A teacher from Montgomery came at the same time, and she say she couldn't let them know she was coming to Highlander, because if these white people knew then she would have lost her job."

"Anyway, Rosa got up and told the group about it. We had somebody there from the U.N., and they said to her, 'If anything happens, you get in touch with me, and I'll be sure to see that you have your rights.'"

"After the workshop, Rosa was afraid to go from Highlander to Atlanta. Myles sent me with her. She was afraid that somebody had already spoken, and she didn't know what was going to happen. I went with her to Atlanta and saw her in a bus going down to Montgomery. She felt much better then" (*Ready from Within*, pp. 32–3).

Parks found Clark to be an inspiring mentor. In 1981, she reflected, "I am always very much respectful and very much in awe of the presence of Septima Clark, because her life story makes the effort that I have made every minute. I only hope that there is a possible chance that some of her great courage and dignity and wisdom has rubbed off on me. When I first met her in 1955 at Highlander, when I saw how well she could organize and hold things together in this very informal setting of interracial living, I had to admire this great woman. . . . [W]hile on the other hand, I was just the opposite. I was tense, and I was nervous, and I was upset most of the time. . . . However, I was willing to face whatever came, not because I felt that I was going to be benefited or helped personally, because I felt that I had been destroyed too long ago. But I had the hope that the young people would be benefited by equal education, should the decision of 1954 be carried out as it should have been" (*Ready from Within*, pp. 16–17).

When Septima Clark first heard the news of Parks's arrest on the bus, she was incredulous that the shy Rosa she knew at Highlander had found the courage to stand up to white authorities. Clark knew that Parks had not planned that action at Highlander; at the last meeting she had said that she didn't expect much would happen in the cradle of the Confederacy, but she had promised to keep working with the youth (*Ready from Within*, pp. 33–4).

When Parks was brought out from behind bars after bail had been posted, the first person she encountered was Virginia Durr. Parks remembered that "Mrs. Durr was the first person I saw as I came through the iron mesh door with matrons on either side of me. There were tears in her eyes, and she seemed shaken, probably wondering what they had done to me. As soon as they released me, she put her arms around me, and hugged and kissed me as if we were sisters" (*My Life*, pp. 122–3).

Durr remembered, "They brought Mrs. Parks out from behind the bars. That was a terrible sight to me to see this gentle, lovely, sweet woman, whom I knew and was so fond of, being brought down by a matron. She wasn't in handcuffs, but they had to unlock two or three doors that grated loudly. She was very calm. I asked her how they had treated her, and she said, 'Very nicely.' Just at that moment her husband arrived. He was very excited and upset. She went home with him in the car some friend had brought. We told her we would follow her home in Mr. Nixon's car and would discuss the case in her apartment" (*Outside the Magic Circle*, p. 280).

A few weeks later Durr wrote to Myles Horton about Parks: "When she came back [from Highlander] she was so happy and felt so liberated and then as time went on she said the discrimination got worse and worse to bear AFTER having, for the first time in her life, been free of it at Highlander. I am sure that had a lot to do with her daring to risk arrest as she is naturally a very quiet and retiring person, although she has a fierce sense of pride and is in my opinion a really noble woman" (*Daybreak of Freedom*, p. 124).

The bus boycott lasted the entire year, December 1955 to December 1956. Virginia Durr picked up black people who needed a ride, even after the police began to give violation tickets to whites who did this. Many white women picked up the black women who cooked and cleaned for them. The mayor of Montgomery, W.A. "Tacky" Gayle, issued a plea for the white women to stop picking up their maids, but they responded with a roar of indignation. If Tacky Gayle wanted to do their washing, ironing, cleaning, cooking, and looking after their children, they would stop; otherwise, they were going to pick up their maids (*Refusing Racism*, p. 44).

The day following her release, Rosa Parks went to work, by cab, since she decided not to ride the bus again. She continued to work over the Christmas season, but on January 7, 1956, she was "discharged," not because of the boycott, the department store said, but because it was closing the tailor shop in which she worked. She began taking sewing jobs at home, in between meetings and church functions.

The next week a bigger financial blow followed, when Raymond Parks quit his job at Maxwell Air Force Base after his boss prohibited any discussion about the bus boycott or Rosa Parks in the privately owned barbershop. The Parks's white landlord raised their rent $10 a month. Raymond Parks, reduced to answering death threats on the telephone, began drinking heavily and chain-smoking to cope with his depression. Durr wrote to Myles Horton, "It is fine to be a heroine, but the price is high" (*Mine Eyes*, pp. 145–6).

Rosa Parks worked long hours dispatching cab drivers and church station wagons to thirty-two pick-up sites for distributing food and clothing donated from afar. In May and June she went on a speaking and fund-raising tour to New York City, Detroit, and San Francisco, but instead of enjoying the adulation, she began to develop the stomach ulcers that plagued her for years to come. When she returned, she found herself in debt for the first time and eventually had to accept $800 that Durr raised for her (*Mine Eyes*, pp. 165–6; *Daybreak of Freedom*, p. 298).

In early December 1956, Horton invited Parks to return to Highlander to meet with six black students trying to integrate schools in Clinton, Tennessee. Everyone, including Septima Clark, welcomed Parks as a conquering heroine; a week later Horton offered her a full-time job at Highlander, which she refused because her mother did not want to live where there were only white people (*Mine Eyes*, pp. 168–9).

In December 1956, black people resumed riding the buses, sitting where they wished, while whites shot guns into the buses on two occasions. In January 1957, a group of ministers formed the Southern Christian Leadership Conference (SCLC) and elected Rev. King as president. Raymond and Rosa Parks however, continued to receive death threats, and they found no employment in Montgomery. In late July, Rosa Parks called her cousin in Detroit, Thomas Williamson, to tell him of the vicious wording of the latest threat. He advised her to move to Detroit to be safe. Her brother, Sylvester, had also lived there since returning from World War II. Parks was ready to move; the effects of the constant threats on her life and the hopelessness of employment left her and her husband without recourse.

Her family members helped her to arrange the move, and in the fall of 1957 Raymond and Rosa Parks and her mother left Montgomery.

Before Rosa Parks left, Septima Clark visited her to lend support and rally the local churchwomen to come to Highlander to support citizenship schools. When Clark arrived in Montgomery, she called Virginia Durr from Rev. Abernathy's office. Durr had never met Clark and, eager to know her, invited her to stay at her home. Since Clifford was out of town, Virginia and Clark hoped to spend a quiet evening becoming acquainted.

In her excitement Durr forgot that Abernathy's phone was assuredly tapped. Word of Clark's presence at the Durrs' home was passed to local police members, and all evening motorcycles roared around the Durrs' block threatening the women for breaking the law. At 3:00 A.M., the telephone rang, and a voice who claimed to be the chief of police said that a burglary had been committed at Clifford Durr's office. Would Mrs. Durr please come down to identify the missing items?

"At 3:00 A.M.?" responded the incredulous Mrs. Durr.

Clear that she would not open the door or leave Clark alone no matter what, Durr called her brother-in-law, the head of the local Rotary Club and Chamber of Commerce. He phoned the real chief of police, who was home asleep in his bed. Having revealed the ruse to get her out of the house, Durr then turned her attention to Clark, who had awakened and calmly sat reading *The Souls of Black Folk* (interview with Virginia Durr, December 7, 1980).

Virginia Durr found Septima Clark to be a harmonious

person, whose presence soothed one's soul and whose security was based on unfailing self-respect. Composed as could be, Clark had been through much worse than motorcycles riding around the block at night. As Clark remembers the experience, "I was really more afraid of riding with Mrs. Durr because she would stop at a green light and powder her face, and then when the red light came on, she'd go shooting through. I said, 'I'm really more afraid of riding with you than I am of those Klansmen,' because I was so afraid the policeman was going to stop her. Knowing her, of course, they would have gotten me. But we got those women at that workshop to feel as if they could come to Highlander. They brought a group up to Highlander, and we really were able to work quite a bit in Rosa's behalf, which is what we intended to do" (interviews with Septima Clark, August 27–September 2, 1979).

Difficult as it was to be friends even while Parks was in Montgomery, the three women managed to stay in touch after she moved away. Durr became a member of the National Organization for Women, and when they had their first meeting in Washington, D.C., in 1958, she invited Clark to attend and talk about black and white women in the South who didn't dare speak out. Parks and Clark saw each other at SCLC meetings and conventions and re-united in Oakland and Berkeley in 1981. All three women were able to gather at Highlander in October 1982 to celebrate its fiftieth anniversary.

After 1957, Mrs. Clark developed citizenship schools from her base at Highlander until they were transferred to SCLC, when she worked from Atlanta. She gave up her travels and retired in 1970, then took care of her sister and served two terms on the school board of Charleston County. She died on December 15, 1987, and was hailed at her funeral as the "queen mother" of the Civil Rights Movement. Mrs. Parks attended and told reporters that the one thing she remembered about Mrs. Clark was that "she had tremendous patience and endurance. In spite of the obstacles she was confronted with, she never wavered" (*Charleston Post/Courier,* December 20, 1987, p. 1A).

After 1957, Mrs. Durr continued to live in the eye of the storm in Montgomery. Clifford Durr defended cases of white people who violated segregation laws, the biggest involving a sociology professor and fifteen students from a Methodist college in Jacksonville, Illinois, who were arrested for eating in a black restaurant. Virginia hosted many Northern supporters of the Student Non-Violent Coordinating Committee (SNCC) who stopped to spend the night on their way to Mississippi. In May 1961, a busload of Freedom Riders arrived in Montgomery, and local officials stood back for half an hour to give an ordinary crowd of Saturday shoppers time to beat them up. Virginia had nightmares for a long time afterward. In 1964, Clifford Durr retired from practicing law and five years later he and Virginia moved to their farm fifteen miles out of town. After Clifford's death in 1975, Virginia traveled and spoke widely, remained active in state and local politics, and celebrated her ninetieth birthday at Martha's Vineyard, where a daughter had a summer home. When Durr died in 1999 at age ninety-five, President Clinton said that her "courage and steely conviction in the earliest days of the civil rights movement helped to change this nation forever." Parks wrote to her family as if she were writing to Virginia: "We still have a long ways to go, but you, my friend, have made it easier for all of us" (*Refusing Racism*, pp. 46–50).

Rosa Parks outlived her friends. She worked for five years in Detroit as a seamstress in a small, downtown shop, riding the bus to work. She was paid $.75 for each piece of work she completed. She frequently attended SCLC and NAACP meetings. She saw Clark and other civil rights leaders at the March on Washington for jobs and freedom in August 1963, but she did not speak publicly—the SCLC men did not allow any women to speak, only Marian Anderson and Mahalia Jackson were allowed to sing. Parks helped John Conyers win election to the U.S. House of Representatives and worked on his staff from 1965 until she retired in 1988. She became a deaconess in her St. Matthew AME church. She returned to Montgomery in 1965 to march from Selma to Montgomery and in 1975 to celebrate the twentieth anniversary of the bus boycott. Her husband died of cancer in 1977, her brother three months later, and her mother died in 1979. Eight years later she founded the Rosa and Raymond Parks Institute for Self-Development to teach eleven- to seventeen-year-olds how to live with honor. In the 1990s she published three autobiographical books. Surviving an episode of unconsciousness in 1998, Mrs. Parks has reached her nineties.

These remarkable women, Virginia Durr, Septima Clark, and Rosa Parks, could be called perfect Southern women, except that they refused to accept the social world they found. None of them was able to finish college, as they all wished to, nor have the careers they might have had today. Instead, they devoted themselves to community and political work, and to friendships; in the end, supported by each other, they each contributed significantly to overturning the social structure of their region.

Sources

Brinkley, Douglas, *Mine Eyes Have Seen the Glory: The Life of Rosa Parks*. London: Weidenfeld and Nicolson, 2000.

Brown, Cynthia Stokes. *Refusing Racism: White Allies and the Struggle for Civil Rights*. New York: Teachers College Press, 2002.

Burns, Stewart, ed. *Daybreak of Freedom: The Montgomery Bus Boycott*. Chapel Hill, NC: University of North Carolina Press, 1997.

Clark, Septima. *Ready from Within: Septima Clark and the Civil Rights Movement*. Edited by Cynthia Stokes Brown. Navarro, CA: Wild Trees Press, 1986.

Durr, Virginia. *Outside the Magic Circle: The Autobiography of Virginia Foster Durr*. Edited by Hollinger F. Barnard. Tuscaloosa, AL: University of Alabama Press, 1985.

Parks, Rosa, with Jim Haskins. *Rosa Parks: My Story*. New York: Dial, 1992.